Regulation and In-house Lawyers

Other titles available from Law Society Publishing:

SRA Standards and Regulations, November 2019 edition
Solicitors Regulation Authority

Compliance and Ethics in Law Firms, 2nd edition
Tracey Calvert

The Solicitor's Handbook 2019
Gregory Treverton-Jones QC, Nigel West, Susanna Heley and Robert Forman

Data Protection Toolkit, 2nd edition
Alison Matthews

Anti-Money Laundering Toolkit, 2nd edition
Alison Matthews

Titles from Law Society Publishing can be ordered from all good bookshops or direct (telephone 0370 850 1422, or visit our online shop at **www.lawsociety.org.uk/bookshop**).

REGULATION AND IN-HOUSE LAWYERS

A Compliance Guide

SECOND EDITION

Tracey Calvert and Bronwen Still

The Law Society

ISBN-13: 978-1-78446-112-6

First edition published in 2013

This edition published in 2020 by the Law Society
113 Chancery Lane, London WC2A 1PL

Typeset by Columns Design XML Ltd, Reading
Printed by Hobbs the Printers Ltd, Totton, Hants

The paper used for the text pages of this book is FSC® certified. FSC (the Forest Stewardship Council®) is an international network to promote responsible management of the world's forests.

FSC
www.fsc.org
MIX
Paper from responsible sources
FSC® C020438

Contents

Foreword

This is the second edition of this book and has been written to reflect the changes introduced with the SRA Standards and Regulation.

Traditionally, solicitors employed in-house have been restricted to acting for their employer or other individuals and entities closely associated with them but the SRA Standards and Regulations, enacted on 25 November 2019, means many of those restrictions have been removed, including those on in-house lawyers providing non-reserved legal activities to the public.

The Standards and Regulations include new Principles and a new Code of Conduct for Solicitors, RELs and RFLs. These both apply to all solicitors and include mandatory requirements with which in-house solicitors are required to comply.

As an in-house practitioner, you are expected to exercise judgement in applying these standards to the situations you are in and deciding on a course of action depending on your role and responsibilities, your areas of practice, and the nature of your clients.

Understandably, there has been some confusion and worry among our in-house members about the new regime and this book has been designed to bring clarity to the regulatory requirements for in-house lawyers.

Much of the content within it is informed by first-hand information gleaned through training in-house members of the profession and it will answer many of those questions you may have around regulation and assist you in understanding the new ways of practising.

The book outlines how the SRA Standards and Regulations will apply to in-house solicitors and helps you to identify the practical changes you may need to ensure compliance with the requirements of the new SRA regulatory landscape.

I highly recommend it – I know you will find it extremely useful.

Pearl Moses, Head of Risk and Compliance
The Law Society of England and Wales

Acknowledgements

We would like to thank various people who have offered assistance to us whilst we have been writing both editions of this book. They include former colleagues at the Solicitors Regulation Authority, including members of the Professional Ethics Guidance Team, the Policy Team, and Law Society colleagues and the Lexcel team.

Table of cases

Table of statutes

Table of statutory instruments

Table of other enactments

Abbreviations

ABS	alternative business structure
ACAS	Advisory, Conciliation and Arbitration Service
ADR	alternative dispute resolution
AML	anti-money laundering
C&I	Commerce & Industry Group
CDD	client due diligence
CILEx	Chartered Institute of Legal Executives
CLC	Council for Licensed Conveyancers
Code for Firms	SRA Code of Conduct for Firms
Code for Individuals	SRA Code of Conduct for Solicitors, RELs and RFLs
COFA	Compliance Officer for Finance and Administration
COLP	Compliance Officer for Legal Practice
CPD	continuing professional development
CSR	corporate social responsibility
DBS	Disclosure and Barring Service
DPO	Data Protection Officer
FCA	Financial Conduct Authority
FPO 2005	Financial Services and Markets Act 2000 (Financial Promotion) Order 2005
FSMA 2000	Financial Services and Markets Act 2000
GDPR	General Data Protection Regulation
ICAEW	Institute of Chartered Accountants in England and Wales
IPReg	Intellectual Property Regulation Board
JLD	Junior Lawyers Division
LAA	Legal Aid Agency
LASPO 2012	Legal Aid, Sentencing and Punishment of Offenders Act 2012
LeO	Legal Ombudsman
LLG	Lawyers in Local Government
LLP	limited liability partnership
LSA 2007	Legal Services Act 2007
LSB	Legal Services Board
MCQ	Magistrates Court Qualification

MLR	Money Laundering, Terrorist Financing and Transfer of Funds (Information on the Payer) Regulations 2017 (as amended)
MLRO	money laundering reporting officer
MQM	Family Mediation Quality Mark
NCA	National Crime Agency
OFT	Office of Fair Trading
OISC	Office of the Immigration Services Commissioner
POCA 2002	Proceeds of Crime Act 2002
PRA	Prudential Regulation Authority
PSQ	Police Station Qualification
QMB	Quality Mark for the Bar
RAO 2001	Financial Services and Markets Act (Regulated Activities) Order 2001
REL	registered European lawyer
RFL	registered foreign lawyer
SA 1974	Solicitors Act 1974
SDT	Solicitors Disciplinary Tribunal
SQM	Specialist Quality Mark
SRA	Solicitors Regulation Authority
TPMA	third-party managed account
UAE	United Arab Emirates

CHAPTER 1

Introduction

Just when solicitors were becoming reasonably confident they understood their obligations arising from the outcomes-focused, risk-based Solicitors Regulation Authority (SRA) Handbook introduced in 2011, the regulatory wheel has turned again, with the introduction of a new rulebook called SRA Standards and Regulations.[1] In replacing the Handbook, the SRA has sought to maintain high-level ethical standards while giving greater flexibility for innovative service delivery. It has cut out what it now regards as unnecessary regulation and reduced its rules from approximately 500 pages to 150 pages. One of the aims has been to 'future proof' the rules so that over the coming years they will require little alteration, in contrast to the Handbook which had been updated 21 times over a space of eight years.

Of particular interest to in-house lawyers is the repeal of the SRA Practice Framework Rules, which restricted for whom in-house lawyers could act – allowing them to act only for their employer and certain related bodies or individuals. The consequences of this change are significant. It will permit a new type of in-house lawyer, who will be able to provide legal services to the public provided those services are non-reserved. To give a few examples, a solicitor could be employed by a will writing company, bank, or consumer organisation, to provide legal services to the employer's customers. While this will open up the legal services market and provide many new opportunities for in-house practice, there will be associated risks for those involved. This, and the other changes introduced by the new Standards and Regulations, will be explored in detail in this updated edition of *Regulation and In-house Lawyers.*

The SRA's latest bonfire of rules has not been without its critics. The difficulty for the SRA lies in trying to balance the need to encourage innovation, access to justice and competition in legal services (as required by the Legal Services Act (LSA) 2007) against necessary public protections (also required by the Act). Pitching the correct level of public protection in a set of rules is always difficult, and this requirement changes over time as the public becomes more aware of how the legal

1 To ensure you are relying upon the correct version and most up-to-date version of the SRA Standards and Regulations, please refer to **www.sra.org.uk/solicitors/standards-regulations**. In this book, the use of italic in extracts from the SRA Standards and Regulations indicates defined terms from the SRA Glossary (**www.sra.org.uk/solicitors/standards-regulations/glossary**).

services market operates. However, the Law Society and others have been very critical of the SRA's decision to allow solicitors employed by unregulated commercial organisations to offer services to the public, arguing that this could be a step too far and that members of the public could easily be confused into thinking that because they are being advised by a solicitor, they will have all the protections of a regulated firm. The next few years will undoubtedly begin to show whether such concerns were justified.

1.1 BACKGROUND

In-house solicitors holding practising certificates made up 22.4 per cent of the profession as at 31 July 2018 (Law Society, *Annual Statistics Report 2018*). This percentage has remained reasonably constant over the last few years. As has been the case for many years, in-house solicitors work in a variety of environments: local government, central government, quangos, trade and membership associations, commercial organisations, non-commercial organisations such as law centres and charities, and many other entities which are not private practice and which are not authorised and regulated by the SRA. Most work entirely for their employer and its related bodies and will no doubt continue to do so.

In-house lawyers have traditionally had a long-distance relationship with the SRA, working for their employers and little troubled by SRA intervention. The biggest debate with the SRA has often been over whether it is necessary for an in-house solicitor to hold a practising certificate. This is not to say that there cannot be tensions between the wishes of employers and their in-house lawyers over compliance issues, as questions raised with the SRA's ethics advice line reveal. Examples include:

- What should I do if I am employed as a solicitor but my employer expects me to pay for a practising certificate?
- What should I do if I am placed in a position where I am breaching contractual duties owed to my employer to achieve conduct outcomes?
- What do I do if my employer wants me to act for a third party and this places me in breach of SRA regulatory requirements?
- My union has called a strike. What is my position with regard to my ethical duties to my employer?

However, things have changed with the new Standards and Regulations. The repeal of rule 4 of the Practice Framework Rules, allowing lawyers to be employed to provide legal services to the public, is the obvious example and this will be subject to considerable scrutiny. However, the introduction of two Codes of Conduct – one for firms (SRA Code of Conduct for Firms) and the other for individuals (SRA Code of Conduct for Solicitors, RELs and RFLs) is another example of change which will have an impact on in-house practice. In-house solicitors will be required to comply with the Code for Individuals, which is stated to apply 'irrespective of your role or the environment or organisation in which you work'. Circumstances will dictate that certain sections of the Code will not apply to some in-house forms of practice but most sections will apply to those providing services to the public.

What is sure to change is that in-house lawyers who provide services to the public, particularly those employed by commercial organisations, are likely to attract significant attention from the SRA. Their situation will be examined in detail in **Chapter 7**. Whether the new Standards and Regulations will direct more SRA attention to traditional in-house roles remains to be seen, although it would appear unlikely.

This book is aimed at all employed, or in-house, solicitors, registered European lawyers (RELs) and trainee solicitors (collectively referred to throughout the book as 'in-house lawyers'), regardless of their work or their role within their organisation. It describes statutory and regulatory compliance issues, including a tailored analysis of how the new Standards and Regulations should be interpreted by all those who work in-house. It also looks back to the changes introduced by LSA 2007 which continue to have an impact on some employed solicitors and their employers. Where appropriate, case studies and practical examples are included to illustrate these requirements.

1.2 LEGAL SERVICES ACT 2007 – THE BACKDROP TO ALL REGULATORY ACTIVITY

The legal landscape changed dramatically with the introduction of LSA 2007. An SRA executive director described the changes as navigating through a 'brave new world', saying that this quote from *The Tempest* 'hits that nail on the head in describing the progress, change and innovation that has underpinned the significant marketplace and regulatory changes ushered through by the Legal Services Act' (Samantha Barrass, December 2011). These changes continue to resonate, as has been seen through the SRA Handbook and its many updates (as of 6 December 2018, 21 versions had been published). For this reason, it is helpful to look at how LSA 2007 has moulded the development of legal services and the way they are regulated.

The Act was drafted in response to the Clementi Review of the Regulatory Framework for Legal Services in England and Wales. This Review was tasked with considering what regulatory framework would facilitate competition, innovation and the public and consumer interest in an efficient, effective and independent legal sector and to recommend a framework which would be independent, comprehensive, accountable, consistent, flexible, transparent, but proportionate and designed to promote the public interest.

The Review was published in 2004 and drew three main conclusions:

1. There existed an overcomplicated regulatory system with the professional bodies trying – and often failing – to achieve conflicting functions. For

example, the Law Society of England and Wales wore a myriad of hats as it was both the representative and the regulatory body for the solicitors' profession.

2. The handling of service complaints was an in-house function of the professional bodies (in its last guise the Law Society's Legal Complaints Service dealt with complaints about inadequate professional services raised against solicitors and law firms) and consumers suffered a poor service with lengthy delays as a result.
3. The restrictions placed on legal professions in terms of business relationships, management and ownership of legal entities created an anti-competitive environment which prevented the market from developing and stopped innovative methods of providing services from being explored.

The response to these criticisms was LSA 2007 and its fundamental changes. Legal practice and its regulation now look quite different, both for the professional bodies regulating and representing lawyers and for the lawyers themselves.

It is worth recapping the main changes brought about by LSA 2007 as these now underpin all regulatory activity by all legal services regulators. They are:

1. The creation of an overarching regulator: the Legal Services Board (LSB).
2. The statutory obligation to separate representation from regulation which led to solicitors in England and Wales being represented by the Law Society and regulated by the SRA; for barristers, the Bar Council (representation) and the Bar Standards Board (regulation); for legal executives the Chartered Institute of Legal Executives (CILEx) (representation) and CILEx Professional Standards Limited (regulation); and for the Chartered Institute of Patent Attorneys and Chartered Institute of Trade Mark Attorneys, the Intellectual Property Regulation Board.
3. The creation of approved regulators with statutory powers to regulate one or more of the reserved legal activities. Currently the following are approved regulators:

    - The Law Society of England and Wales (working through the independent regulatory body, the SRA);
    - The Bar Council (through the Bar Standards Board);
    - Chartered Institute of Legal Executives (through CILEx Regulation);
    - Council for Licensed Conveyancers;
    - Chartered Institute of Patent Attorneys and Institute of Trade Mark Attorneys (through the Intellectual Property Regulation Board);
    - Association of Costs Lawyers (through the Costs Lawyers Standards Board);
    - Master of the Faculties;
    - Institute of Chartered Accountants of Scotland (for reserved probate activities only); and

- Association of Chartered Certified Accountants (for reserved probate activities only).

4. The requirement that approved regulators must promote, among those they regulate, the regulatory objectives and the professional principles set out in LSA 2007, s.1. These are discussed below.

1.2.1 Section 1(1) – the regulatory objectives

These are:

- protecting and promoting the public interest;
- supporting the constitutional principle of the rule of law;
- improving access to justice;
- protecting and promoting the interests of consumers;
- promoting competition in the provision of services;
- encouraging an independent, strong, diverse and effective legal profession;
- increasing public understanding of a citizen's legal rights and duties; and
- promoting and maintaining adherence to the professional principles.

1.2.2 Section 1(3) – the professional principles

These are:

- that authorised persons should act with independence and integrity;
- that authorised persons should maintain proper standards of work;
- that authorised persons should act in the best interests of their clients;
- that persons who exercise before any court a right of audience, or conduct litigation in relation to proceedings in any court, by virtue of being authorised persons should comply with their duty to the court to act with independence in the interests of justice; and
- that the affairs of clients should be kept confidential.

In LSA 2007 'authorised persons' means authorised persons in relation to activities which are reserved legal activities, for example solicitors and barristers.

Other fundamental changes included the creation of the Office for Legal Complaints and the Legal Ombudsman, which replaced all other legal complaints handling bodies.

The Legal Services Consumer Panel was also established as an independent arm of the LSB empowered to provide evidence-based advice to the Board which represents the interests of the many different consumers of legal services.

There has also been the promotion of competition in the legal marketplace with the introduction of alternative business structures (ABSs), i.e. legal entities with non-lawyer investment and/or non-lawyer managers, which are licensed to provide reserved legal activities. ABSs, totalling well over 800 (as of early 2019), have been licensed by the SRA since 2012.

1.3 THE SRA'S RESPONSE – THE 2011 HANDBOOK

The SRA response to LSA 2007 was the launch of the SRA Handbook on 6 October 2011, which Charles Plant, Chair of the SRA Board said (at *The Lawyer* conference on alternative business structures, 8 November 2010) 'will bring together all the SRA's regulatory requirements into a single, coherent structure that underpins the regulation of solicitors, law firms and alternative business structures'.

The Handbook was, when launched, in fact much more than simply a collection of rules and regulations. It enabled the newly created SRA to reposition itself as an approved regulator reflecting the requirements of LSA 2007 and the regulatory objectives. Its emphasis was on outcomes-focused and risk-based regulation which focused on entities as much as individuals. Since its introduction it has been subject to continual revision to allow greater innovation in practice through, for example, changes such as the relaxation of the separate business outcomes, which allows solicitors to offer non-reserved legal services through separate businesses.

1.4 OUTCOMES-FOCUSED REGULATION

Outcomes-focused regulation was described by Charles Plant (at *The Lawyer* conference on alternative business structures, 8 November 2010) as follows:

> [Outcomes-focused regulation] is a regulatory regime that focuses on the high level principles and outcomes that should drive the provision of services for clients. It is backed by firm enforcement action where required.
>
> This is in contrast to the previously more prescriptive approach to regulation. This has been replaced with a framework which encourages flexibility in approach where this is both safe and in the public interest.

The 2011 Handbook used outcomes in two ways. First, all the regulatory requirements, expressed as rules and regulations in the Handbook, were prefaced with outcomes which explained the purpose of the requirements and how they supported the regulatory objectives and professional principles in LSA 2007.

For example, the SRA Training Regulations 2011 included requirements imposed on those individuals and firms (including those individuals working in-house and authorised to offer training contracts) which provided training for trainee solicitors (in Part 2 (Training Provider Regulations)). The outcome which had to be satisfied was that:

> you should have appropriate systems in place to provide the required level and quality of training, and deliver that training effectively.

Second, the SRA Code of Conduct 2011 was expressed as a completely outcomes-focused set of requirements in the SRA Handbook and as a consequence looked very different from previous codes of conduct. Outcomes replaced prescriptive rules and achieving outcomes meant having to ensure that the right result was obtained for a client. How an outcome was achieved was largely left unexplained, providing scope for flexibility and an element of freedom to work out the best methods to accommodate the needs of individual clients. For in-house lawyers, most outcomes in the Code of Conduct did apply but the relevance of many of the outcomes depended on the circumstances in which they were employed. Most in-house lawyers were untroubled, for example, by the outcomes relating to introductions and referrals.

1.5 RISK-BASED REGULATION

The SRA also changed the way it regulated, to focus on the risks that are of most consequence to clients and the public interest. This was expressed in an SRA strategy statement as follows:

> The public has a right to expect us to focus our resources on the solicitors and firms that are most likely to harm their interests as consumers of legal services, and to act promptly and effectively when risks are identified.

For individuals regulated by the SRA this meant that they were required to take responsibility for identifying those risks which presented themselves because of their type of work, type of client, business model, etc. and they would be expected to put in place systems and controls to mitigate those risks as much as possible. Inevitably, this created much greater anxiety for those in private practice who had responsibility for running a regulated practice, handling client money and meeting client care needs.

For in-house lawyers the need to address risk was less explicitly expressed but existed nonetheless. They needed to consider questions such as: What risks present themselves to you because of the type of work you do and the nature of your employer? Do you have responsibilities to manage a legal team? How would you deal with situations where there might be a conflict of interests because you are asked to represent a fellow employee as well as your employer? How would you be able to minimise those risks?

Obvious examples of risks arising in respect of in-house practice include those associated with both money laundering and mortgage fraud. These are two concerns which the SRA has publicly identified as posing a risk to its reputation as a regulator and the requirement to regulate in the public interest. Therefore, those managing an in-house team for a bank or building society employer should be satisfied that they are adequately managing the risks associated with this. While the SRA has no regulatory authority over the employer, it expects employed solicitors as authorised persons to be aware of, and play a part in managing, such risks.

1.6 ENTITY-BASED REGULATION

The final shift in focus came with the SRA's change of emphasis away from the individuals it regulates to a consideration of the firms, or entities, which it authorises and regulates. Is the entity which carries SRA labelling safe to provide services to the public and safe to be authorised by it? This focus means that the SRA's concern has become increasingly with corporate governance, effective management, and the adoption of proper financial and risk management principles.

This may previously have had little relevance to in-house practice but, with the new Standards and Regulations, in-house solicitors providing services to the public may see attempts by the SRA to regulate their unregulated employer, and the legal services it provides, through the back door, i.e. through regulation of the solicitor. This will be explored in detail later on.

1.7 THE NEW 2019 STANDARDS AND REGULATIONS

These are effective from 25 November 2019. For those in-house lawyers providing services to the public, three separate pieces of SRA guidance have been published to help them better understand what is expected of them and of their employer. Guidance has also been published by the Law Society on this new form of practice. The rest of this book will consider the new rules and guidance and their likely impact on all aspects of in-house practice.

CHAPTER 2

Making the move into in-house practice – what you should know

2.1 INTRODUCTION

Many solicitors spend all their working lives either working in private practice or working in-house in one capacity or another. However, many solicitors are making the switch from private practice to in-house, as is demonstrated by the year-on-year increase in the number of practising solicitors working in this area.

In-house practice offers a number of benefits to a lawyer: flexibility of working life and variety in work are two obvious attractions. Non-solicitor employers can see many benefits in employing lawyers, and employing someone legally qualified in a commercial or business environment can enhance the employer's reputation through the lawyer's adherence to certain professional ethics, such as acting in the best interests of clients. Lawyers acting in public fields are often able to provide their employers with a broad overview of the wider implications of particular instructions.

Also, the scope to diversify within an in-house environment, particularly in commercial organisations, may be easier than in private practice where it is expected that the more senior the individual, the more specialised they will become in the areas of law which they practise.

2.2 KEY DISTINCTIONS

There are a number of differences between private practice and in-house practice and it is vital that anyone making the move understands the key distinctions. These are shown in Table 2.1.

Table 2.1 Key distinctions between private practice and in-house practice

Private practice	In-house practice	Don't forget the following points
Able to act for any clients.	You can provide advice to your employer and related bodies.	Broadly, your employer is your primary client. While this may mean that when acting for your employer you can dispense with client care letters and costs information, it is still essential to agree terms of instructions and properly record these and be satisfied that you have the competence to act. Failure to do this may create tensions between you and your employer and will not provide you with an accurate record of what has been agreed. In other words, acting in-house does not mean file maintenance should be anything less than what would be expected as good practice in a private practice environment.

Private practice	In-house practice	Don't forget the following points
	You can also provide legal advice to external clients provided that your services do *not* include any of the following restricted activities: (1) Reserved legal activities to the public or a section of the public. (2) Immigration work (unless your employer is separately authorised by the Office of the Immigration Service Commissioner). (3) Claims management services (unless your employer is authorised by the Financial Conduct Authority (FCA)). (4) Financial services activities that require authorisation by the FCA (except where your employer is FCA-authorised).	In circumstances where you are providing services to clients other than your employer, it will be necessary to comply with regulatory standards, etc. While your employer is not authorised by the SRA, you are, and you must comply with the SRA Principles and SRA Code of Conduct for Solicitors, RELs and RFLs (the Code for Individuals) and all other relevant requirements in the SRA Standards and Regulations. In particular, the duties in respect of paragraphs 8.1–8.11 in the Code for Individuals. Client information would extend to ensuring that the client understands what (if any) regulatory protections are available to them and explaining that your employer is not regulated by the SRA.
You must also consider your conduct duties and not act in any circumstances where to do so would breach your personal obligations.	There is no difference in in-house practice and it will be a personal obligation to ensure that you can reconcile conduct obligations with what is required of you under the terms of your employment contract.	You must be satisfied that your personal duties as a lawyer are reconcilable with your employment duties. For example, are you being asked to act in a conflict? Are you able to ensure confidentiality owed to your employer is upheld? Make sure that the terms of your contract do not contradict your regulatory duties.

Private practice	In-house practice	Don't forget the following points
You must always hold a current practising certificate.	There is a discretion not to hold a practising certificate, but its application is narrow and you might be committing a criminal offence if you misinterpret the requirement.	You must be confident that you have made the correct judgment about whether you need a practising certificate. Check your employment contract, job title, what you are expected to do, your responsibilities, etc. and regardless of your employer's views, make the right decision to avoid a criminal offence and regulatory issues.
You will be employed – usually – to perform legal services in a particular area of law.	You are more likely – particularly if newly qualified – to be performing a variety of legal services, being regarded as a generalist rather than a specialist.	Make sure that you have the competence to perform such a variety of legal services and, if not, be prepared to say that you cannot act for the employer in a particular retainer. To act without the necessary competence would mean that you are not achieving the service standards expected of you in section 3 of the Code for Individuals, may create employment difficulties, and may jeopardise your employer's position. In other words, know the limit of your capabilities and do not be afraid to say no to your employer.
You usually do not have a role in corporate matters unless you are a manager (partner, director, member) of the firm.	You may be expected to advise on corporate governance, regulatory risks, and other business management issues.	Make sure you have the competence to give such advice and that you are able to give unfettered, independent advice to the board/senior officials with access to the right people and the right information. You will be expected to provide an independent overview.

Private practice	In-house practice	Don't forget the following points
It is unlikely that you would be expected to manage a team of lawyers without having demonstrated your experience to the managers.	You may be expected to manage a legal team despite a lack of proven ability in the skills which are needed.	Again, are you confident that you have the appropriate skills, know your staff and their capabilities, have the resources for supervision and training, and have access to senior members of the organisation should you have any concerns? Anything less than this may have an impact on your employment and may make you answerable for the actions of members of the team. Bear in mind also the SRA's requirement, as expressed in paragraphs 3.5 and 3.6 of the Code for Individuals, about personal accountability for the actions of those you manage and/or supervise.

Private practice	In-house practice	Don't forget the following points
The firm must have compulsory professional indemnity insurance which covers your acts and defaults.	A non-solicitor employer is not required to have professional indemnity insurance for the SRA's purposes. You may be exposed to negligence claims brought against you by both your employer and others.	Make sure that you have the conversation with your employer about your position and consider whether there is a need to have appropriate indemnity insurance to protect yourself. In commerce and industry, would it be possible to have directors' and officers' liability insurance? When providing reserved legal services to members of the public from a non-commercial body (a not-for-profit body, a community interest group or an independent trade union) you are obliged to comply with the Code for Individuals, paragraph 5.6, which states that you must ensure that your employer takes out and maintains adequate and appropriate indemnity cover in respect of the services you provide. The SRA has issued guidance to assist with this ('Adequate and appropriate indemnity insurance' – September 2019: **www.sra.org.uk/solicitors/guidance/ethics-guidance/adequate-and-appropriate-indemnity-insurance**). In other circumstances, when providing services to external clients, bear in mind the need to comply with the Code for Individuals and provide clients with the information about the regulatory protections available to them.

Private practice	In-house practice	Don't forget the following points
If you give an undertaking in private practice, during the course of your work, the managers of the firm will be bound to comply with it.	In in-house practice you are personally bound by undertakings given in the course of your professional duties.	Make sure you are satisfied that you understand your employer's attitude to undertakings and that you exercise risk management tactics in respect of the giving, recording, discharging and release from undertakings. Undertakings issues can have an impact on your employment and also be a regulatory issue.
You must comply with the SRA Accounts Rules if you hold client money, and in certain other circumstances.	You are not allowed to personally hold client money unless you work for an authorised body or in an organisation prescribed by the SRA as being able to hold client money.	This creates personal obligations so make sure that your employer is aware of the situation and accommodates the measures which are necessary to comply. You cannot personally hold client money, but your business is able to hold money belonging to a client and you can be a signatory to your employer's bank account. The client in these circumstances must be advised of the relevant information about the type of account.

CHAPTER 3

The need for a practising certificate

3.1 INTRODUCTION

The need for a practising certificate for individuals who are on the roll of solicitors and working in private practice is generally well understood. However, there are many more misunderstandings about the position of individuals who are admitted to the roll and working in-house for non-solicitor employers. As a consequence of this, many myths have developed about the supposed ability to practise as a solicitor in such circumstances without a practising certificate.

Whether you are moving into an in-house position from private practice, or have always held an in-house role, you will need a very good understanding of the importance of your job title, the role specification and how you are described, or 'held out', by your employer and colleagues. All these considerations are connected with the issue of whether or not you must hold a practising certificate.

In fact, the ability to practise as a solicitor without a current practising certificate is very limited, and great caution should be exercised when deciding whether an individual's particular circumstances would enable them to practise in this way. This is because the need for a practising certificate is a statutory obligation contained in the Solicitors Act (SA) 1974 (as amended by LSA 2007). You will be subject to regulatory scrutiny if you commit an offence under SA 1974 as this would be considered a breach of the SRA Code of Conduct for Solicitors, RELs and RFLs, paragraph 7.1, and your duty to 'keep up to date with and follow the law and regulation governing the way you work'.

3.2 THE STATUTORY OBLIGATIONS

SOLICITORS ACT 1974

1. Qualifications for practising as solicitor

No person shall be qualified to act as a solicitor unless –

(a) he has been admitted as a solicitor, and
(b) his name is on the roll, and

(c) he has in force a certificate issued by the Society in accordance with the provisions of this Part authorising him to practise as a solicitor (in this Act referred to as a 'practising certificate').

If you practise as a solicitor, in private practice or in-house, without having a current practising certificate you will be both committing a criminal offence under SA 1974, s.21 and breaching the SRA's Standards and Regulations, unless you can rely on the exemption in SA 1974, s.88.

3.3 THE SECTION 88 EXEMPTION

SOLICITORS ACT 1974

88. Saving for solicitors to public departments and City of London

(1) Nothing in this Act shall prejudice or affect any rights or privileges of the solicitor to the Treasury, any other public department, the Church Commissioners or the Duchy of Cornwall, or require any such officer or any clerk or officer appointed to act for him to be admitted or enrolled or to hold a practising certificate in any case where it would not have been necessary for him to be admitted or enrolled or to hold such a certificate if this Act had not been passed.

(1A) The exemption from the requirement to hold a practising certificate conferred by subsection (1) above shall not apply to solicitors who are Crown Prosecutors.

(2) Sections 31 and 32(1) shall not apply to, and nothing in this Act shall prejudice or affect any rights or privileges which immediately before the commencement of this Act attached to the office of, the Solicitor of the City of London.

SA 1974, s.88 enables solicitors working in certain public departments, and any clerk or officer appointed to work for them who are able to rely on this statutory exemption, to be able to practise without a certificate.

However, confusion abounds because of the lack of elaboration as to the meaning of the section. The most recent view of the SRA Board, as published in the Solicitors' Code of Conduct 2007, is that individuals are able to rely on this exemption if they hold the office of principal solicitor to:

- the Treasury;
- any other public department;
- the Church Commissioners;
- the Duchy of Cornwall;

or if they are a solicitor who is appointed as a clerk or officer to any of these principal solicitors.

Similarly, there is a lack of explanation in SA 1974 of the term 'public department'. The SRA has previously expressed the view that this would include any department of central government in the UK, the National Assembly for Wales and any non-ministerial departments. The Board's present view is that the exemption does not apply to solicitors working for other agencies or any non-departmental public body.

The Cabinet Office maintains records of departments, agencies and public bodies and gives the following as examples of non-ministerial departments (**www.gov.uk/government/organisations**):

- The Charity Commission;
- Government Legal Department;
- HM Land Registry;
- HM Revenue & Customs;
- National Crime Agency;
- Serious Fraud Office;
- Supreme Court of the United Kingdom; and
- UK Statistics Authority.

Similarly, the Cabinet Office data lists non-departmental public bodies and other agencies and advisory bodies. Taking the present view of the SRA Board, it seems highly unlikely that solicitors working for such organisations would be able to rely on the s.88 exemption.

Examples include the following:

- Highways Agency;
- UK Border Force;
- HM Courts & Tribunals Service;
- Arts Council England;
- Environment Agency; and
- Boundary Commission.

It is therefore clear that great care must be exercised when relying on the s.88 exemption in relation to practice.

Even if it can be used, the exemption relates exclusively to the capacity and employment of the solicitor and it cannot be used to cover any other form of employment or activities. For example, solicitors working in non-ministerial departments without practising certificates cannot in these circumstances administer an oath. Similarly, individuals can be described as solicitors in relation to their s.88 employment (e.g. on their in-house notepaper) but not in relation to work undertaken outside that employment which would require them to hold a practising certificate.

As the exemption is a statutory one, the onus will be on the individual concerned to ensure that they are entitled to rely on it. Solicitors should consider whether it would be prudent to seek legal advice to support their decision to rely on the exemption. If challenged by the SRA, the individual would be expected to demonstrate the steps they had taken to satisfy themselves on the point.

3.4 OTHER IN-HOUSE ROLES

Unless an individual working as a lawyer in an in-house position can rely on the fairly limited statutory exemption in SA 1974, s.88, that individual will be practising as a solicitor and will need a practising certificate in the situations described below.

1. If they are employed as a solicitor, which is likely to arise in the following circumstances:

   - An individual is on the roll of solicitors and is explicitly employed as a practising solicitor with a job title which includes such terms as solicitor, lawyer, counsel, attorney or legal practitioner. These titles imply that the individual has a professional qualification as a lawyer and this assumption cannot be negated by use of additional wording such as 'non-practising'.
   - Where it is a requirement of the job that the office holder is a qualified lawyer. This means that regardless of their job title, individuals are likely to be holding themselves out as solicitors as this is a requirement of their job description and/or they are employed in a legal department to undertake the legal work of that department or a substantial part of their job involves activities of the kind usually undertaken by solicitors. If there are any concerns that a solicitor is employed in such circumstances, the SRA is likely to pay close attention to the person's job description, the person specification for the role and/or the person's contract of employment.

2. If they are held out, explicitly or implicitly, as a solicitor, which is likely to arise in the following circumstances:

   - If the individual is described (in contrast to the use of such wording as part of a job title) as a solicitor, lawyer or attorney. This assumption can only be negated by making it clear that the term is being used to describe a qualification of another jurisdiction (for example, 'Australian solicitor') or it is made clear that the individual is not practising by qualifying the description by words such as 'non-practising' or 'retired' (for example, 'chief legal officer and non-practising solicitor'). Having said that, certain descriptions, such as 'lawyer', cannot be negated by, for example, the description 'non-practising solicitor'. The following provides examples of descriptions which can be negated and those which cannot.

     Descriptions which can be negated by adding words such as 'non-practising solicitor' or 'retired solicitor':

     – Chief legal officer;
     – Director of legal services;

- Head of legal affairs;
- Legal adviser;
- Legal and business consultant;
- Legal director;
- Legal expert;
- Legal and HR director.

Descriptions which cannot be negated:

- Solicitor;
- Lawyer;
- Counsel;
- Attorney;
- Legal practitioner.

- Being described on stationery, or other publicity for the employer, as being a member of the Law Society implicitly holds out the individual as being a practising solicitor unless this is otherwise negated.

3. In limited circumstances, where an individual fulfils an in-house supervisory role and, as part of the person's employment, the department carries on publicly funded work or the individual does or supervises advocacy or the conduct of proceedings for members of the public before a court or immigration tribunal.
4. In other circumstances, an individual may require a practising certificate because of the activities which they undertake either in a personal capacity or because of the requirements of their employment. This would include the following:
   - the individual personally administers oaths;
   - the individual appears before a court or tribunal in reliance upon having a qualification as a solicitor;
   - the individual instructs counsel; and
   - the individual does reserved work or provides immigration services in their own right, or they are responsible for supervising unqualified staff who undertake reserved work.

3.5 RESERVED LEGAL ACTIVITIES

The need for a practising certificate (see Figure 3.1 below) is connected with the ability to carry on reserved legal activities by way of business. The meaning of this phrase is now contained in LSA 2007, s.12 and Sched.2. Table 3.1 explains more fully what is meant in relation to the reserved legal activities that can be undertaken by solicitors regulated by the SRA in its capacity as an approved regulator.

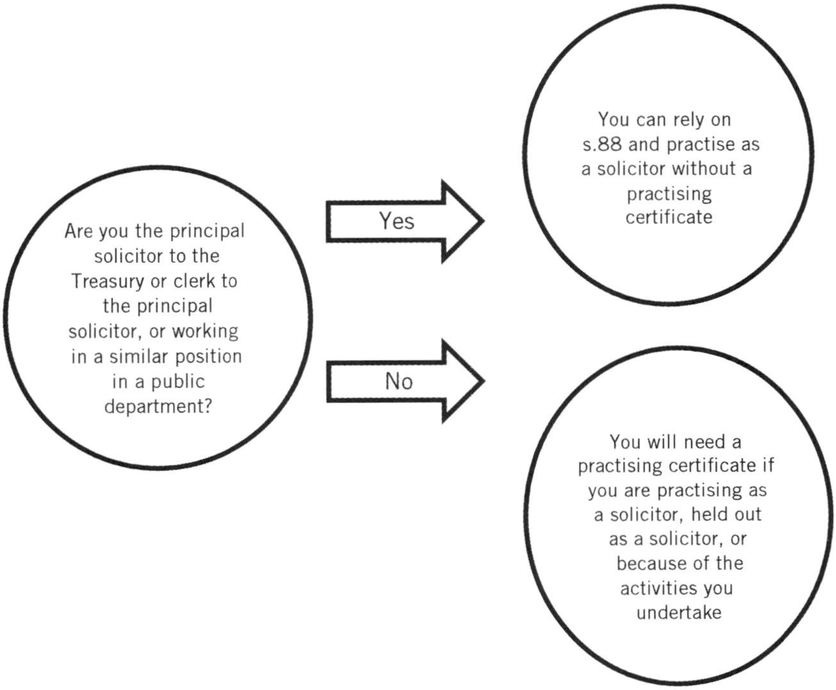

Figure 3.1 Do you need a practising certificate?

Table 3.1 Meaning of reserved legal activities

Reserved legal activity	**Meaning**
The exercise of rights of audience	The right to appear before and address a court, including the right to call and examine witnesses.
The conduct of litigation	The issuing of proceedings before any court in England and Wales; the commencement, prosecution and defence of such proceedings; the performance of any ancillary functions in relation to such proceedings (such as entering appearances to actions).

Reserved legal activity	Meaning
Reserved instrument activities (dealing with the transfer of land or property under specific legal provisions)	Preparing any instrument of transfer or charge for the purposes of the Land Registration Act 2002; making an application or lodging a document for registration under that Act; preparing any other instrument relating to real or personal estate for the purposes of the law of England and Wales or instrument relating to court proceedings in England and Wales. Here, instrument means any contract for sale or other disposition of land except a contract to grant a short lease.
Probate activities	Preparing any probate papers for the purposes of the law of England and Wales or in relation to any proceedings in England and Wales. Probate papers means papers on which to found or oppose a grant of probate or a grant of letters of administration.
The administration of oaths	The exercise of the powers conferred on a commissioner for oaths by the Commissioners for Oaths Act 1889, the Commissioners for Oaths Act 1891 and the Stamp Duties Management Act 1891, s.24.

The SRA expresses the regulatory requirements in the SRA Authorisation of Individuals Regulations. The regulations that are relevant to in-house practice are 9.1, 9.5, 9.6, 9.7, 9.8 and 9.10.

Reserved legal activities

9.1 Subject to regulations 9.2, 9.3, 9.5 to 9.10 and 10.2(b), if you are a *solicitor* with a current practising certificate, or an *REL*, you are entitled to carry on all *reserved legal activities* except notarial activities.

Immigration work

9.5 If you are a *solicitor*, an *REL* or *RFL* you may undertake *immigration work*, provided that such work is undertaken through:

(a) an authorised body;
(b) an authorised non-SRA firm that is a qualified person under the Immigration and Asylum Act 1999; or
(c) a body regulated by the Office of the Immigration Services Commissioner.

9.6 Subject to regulation 9.7, if you are a *solicitor*, an *REL* or *RFL* you may only undertake *immigration work* for the public, or a section of the public, that comprises *reserved legal activities* if such work is undertaken through a body that is entitled to carry on *reserved legal activities* under the *LSA*.

9.7 Regulations 9.5 and 9.6 do not restrict you from undertaking *immigration work* if you fall within section 84(6) of the Immigration and Asylum Act 1999.

Claims management services

9.8 If you are a *solicitor*, an *REL* or *RFL* you may carry on *regulated claims management activities* or activities that would be *regulated claims management activities* but for the exclusion in article 89N of the *Regulated Activities Order*, provided that such work is undertaken through:

(a) a body authorised to carry on *reserved legal activities*; or
(b) if the work does not comprise *reserved legal activities*

(i) a body which has been granted permission to carry on *regulated claims management activities* by the *FCA* under Part 4A of *FSMA*; or
(ii) as permitted under an exemption made in or under *FSMA*, to the general prohibition set out in section 19 of *FSMA*.

Higher rights of audience

9.10 If you are a *solicitor* or an *REL* you may exercise civil or criminal advocacy in the *higher courts* if the *SRA* is satisfied you have successfully and satisfactorily completed the appropriate *higher courts advocacy qualification*, or you are:

(a) an *REL* or *lawyer* to whom Directive 2005/36 applies and you have applied for a qualification to exercise rights of audience in the *higher courts*, and you have undertaken any further steps as the *SRA* specifies in order to gain the qualification; or
(b) authorised by another *approved regulator* to exercise civil or criminal advocacy in the *higher courts*.

3.6 IMMIGRATION WORK

Immigration work – in other words, immigration advice and immigration services – is not a reserved activity. However, it is restricted to certain persons under the Immigration and Asylum Act 1999.

Regulation 9.5 (shown above) of the SRA Authorisation of Individuals Regulations contains an explanation of the position. Immigration services relating to courts or immigration tribunals will fall within the category of reserved activities arising in respect of advocacy and court work. The court work is subject to the normal restriction on court work.

Other immigration work is not reserved work, but can only be done by an authorised person such as a solicitor, barrister, chartered legal executive, member of an Establishment Directive profession, or a registered foreign lawyer practising as such, or under the supervision of an authorised person, or under an exemption given by the Office of the Immigration Services Commissioner (OISC). This position, and the meaning of authorised person, is likely to change depending on the outcome of the Brexit negotiations, and registered European lawyers (RELs) must monitor their position carefully.

Additional information is available from the OISC's website, **www.gov.uk/government/organisations/office-of-the-immigration-services-commissioner**.

3.7 LOCAL GOVERNMENT OFFICERS

An important caveat to the prohibition on reserved legal activities is contained in the Local Government Act 1972, s.223 (as amended by LSA 2007 and other legislation). The relevant section is shown below:

LOCAL GOVERNMENT ACT 1972

223 Appearance of local authorities in legal proceedings.

(1) Any member or officer of a local authority who is authorised by that authority to prosecute or defend on their behalf, or to appear on their behalf in, proceedings before a magistrates' court shall be entitled to prosecute or defend or to appear in any such proceedings, and, to conduct any such proceedings.

(2) In this section 'local authority' includes the Common Council, a joint authority, an economic prosperity board, a combined authority, a joint waste authority, the Greater London Authority and, a police and crime commissioner and the Mayor's Office for Policing and Crime.

This means that advocacy can be undertaken by non-solicitors working for local government departments and also therefore by non-practising solicitors. The latter will, however, need to be satisfied that nothing about their job title, contract of employment or the authority's materials holds them out as a solicitor and that they do not carry on any other reserved legal activities. They will also want to be satisfied that they have been properly authorised as set out in s.223(1) of this Act and that, for their own peace of mind, they have a record of such authorisation.

3.8 REPERCUSSIONS OF PRACTISING UNCERTIFICATED

Practising uncertificated is both a criminal offence and a regulatory concern. There are numerous examples of the repercussions for individuals who make the wrong decision about the need for a practising certificate and who as a consequence are investigated by the SRA and referred to the Solicitors Disciplinary Tribunal (SDT).

3.9 APPLYING FOR A PRACTISING CERTIFICATE

Many solicitors will reach an agreement with their employer that the employer will pay the fee for their practising certificate.

However, regardless of what is negotiated as a term of the individual's employment, the responsibility for holding a current certificate lies with the individual, and the fact that an employer may refuse to pay, or does not agree with the interpretation of the statutory requirements, does not impose any lesser duty on the individual to comply.

The requirements and process are contained in the SRA Authorisation of Individuals Regulations (see **www.sra.org.uk**) in the SRA Standards and Regulations.

It is important to note that individuals are expected to provide the SRA with sufficient information to enable the SRA to make appropriate judgments concerning whether to authorise, or continue to authorise, any person, and that only those individuals who meet the SRA's criteria for authorisation (including the requirements to be suitable and capable of providing legal services to the required standard) are authorised.

The application process is described in reg.6 of the SRA Authorisation of Individuals Regulations as follows:

1. The application must be on the prescribed form. Full information is listed on the SRA website and the correct form is currently designated as the RF3 form for individual applications by solicitors on the roll of solicitors. In some cases the individual must disclose and/or declare certain information about themselves and complete a different application, currently described as a REG3. More details appear below.
2. Payment of the prescribed fee must be made and the correct contribution to the SRA Compensation Fund must also be submitted (see below). The individual practising certificate fee is a flat annual fee levied on all solicitors. The practising certificate year runs from 1 November to 31 October, and the flat fee is reduced depending on the time of the initial application. There is also a reduction for solicitors on maternity leave.
3. Any other information (for example, other documents and references) that the SRA may require must be submitted.

As mentioned at point 1 above, some individuals may need to submit additional information to the SRA. If this applies, the application for a practising certificate must be completed in the prescribed form REG3 and, in situations where the application is not an initial submission, applications must be submitted to renew a practising certificate six weeks in advance of the normal renewal date.

The SRA has the discretion to impose conditions in accordance with reg.7 of the SRA Authorisation of Individuals Regulations or to refuse the application. Such decisions are subject to the right of appeal by the applicant as conferred by the SRA Application, Notice, Review and Appeal Rules.

Applications are now undertaken online, using the SRA's online resource known as 'mySRA'. This requires individuals to activate a personal online account and thereafter make practising certificate applications via this medium. It is also used to update the SRA with other information about the individual including changes to a practising address, etc. A consequence of this method is that solicitors are not issued with paper practising certificates and instead these are stored in a downloadable PDF format on the individual's account. Further information about the system is on the SRA website, **www.sra.org.uk**.

The commencement date for practising certificates is the date on which it is entered in the register of holders of practising certificates as having commenced. The replacement date is the 31 October following the issue of the certificate. The certificate expires:

- when a replacement certificate is issued;
- on the death of the solicitor;
- if the solicitor is removed from or struck off the roll of solicitors;
- in the case of a practising certificate which is suspended, on its replacement date; or
- if its replacement date has passed, 14 days after the suspension took effect.

3.10 SRA COMPENSATION FUND CONTRIBUTIONS

With the exception of solicitors who are employed as Crown Prosecutors, a solicitor with a current practising certificate must make an individual contribution to the SRA Compensation Fund regardless of their type of employment.

An application for a practising certificate must include the prescribed contribution to the Fund.

The Law Society is required to establish and maintain this fund for making discretionary grants in respect of compensation claims to those who have suffered loss because of a solicitor's (or their employee's) dishonesty or where the applicant has suffered hardship because of the solicitor's failure to account for monies due. It is described as a fund of last resort in so far as grants are made where the applicant is not otherwise indemnified against the loss. The Fund is administered through the SRA.

The SRA Compensation Fund Rules are in the SRA Standards and Regulations.

At first glance, it may appear that the application of the SRA Compensation Fund requirements to solicitors working in-house has no significance. However, the SRA Compensation Fund Rules apply to a defaulting practitioner, which is defined in rule 5 as including a solicitor (or Registered European Lawyer) who at the date of the relevant act or omission was practising in an SRA-authorised firm or practising in a non-commercial body. The latter will be a not-for-profit body, a community interest company or an independent trade union.

The current requirement is for each individual applying for a practising certificate to make a flat-fee contribution. This is topped up by way of firm-based contributions from entities authorised and regulated by the SRA and it is this additional contribution from private practice which makes the responsibility to keep the Fund viable more proportionate. While this fact has no relevance to the employers of in-house lawyers, should they decide that it is necessary or desirable to make an application to the SRA to become an ABS then they would be obliged to make such payments to the Fund.

CHAPTER 4

Regulatory compliance – an overview

4.1 INTRODUCTION

Chapter 3 focused on issues arising in respect of statutory obligations, specifically the requirement for those admitted to the roll of solicitors to hold a current practising certificate and the need to be aware that certain legal activities (known as reserved legal activities) can only be carried on in a business environment by certain categories of people, such as solicitors and other qualified lawyers, or under their direct supervision.

Breach of these statutory requirements will be both a legal issue and a regulatory issue.

This chapter looks at regulatory compliance issues and provides an overview of the relevance of the rules and regulations of the SRA for in-house lawyers.

4.2 THE LEGAL SERVICES ACT 2007

Much that has happened in recent years to change the legal landscape is almost wholly due to the Legal Services Act (LSA) 2007, described by the Law Society as 'the biggest reform of the regulation of legal services in England and Wales for a generation' (Law Society, 'The Legal Services Act 2007 – Briefing', 29 November 2007). Although the Act has now been in place for well over a decade, it remains the reference point for all legal services regulators, including the SRA. For this reason, it is still worth reflecting on why it was introduced and its fundamental objectives, as these underpin the SRA's continued direction of travel, culminating in the new Standards and Regulations.

At the turn of the century, the Office of Fair Trading (OFT) published a report entitled 'Competition in the Professions' which supported the removal of anti-competitive and overly restrictive rules in the legal profession. In response, the government commissioned Sir David Clementi, a former deputy governor of the Bank of England, to produce an independent review of the regulatory framework in England and Wales. He conducted a thorough 'root and branch' review of the legal profession in the UK.

This resulted in the Clementi Report, published in 2004, which was the forerunner to LSA 2007. Both the OFT and Clementi reports were critical of the regulation and provision of legal services: key criticisms focused on over-complex and inconsistent regulation, lack of competition in terms of service providers, restrictions on how solicitors could operate, and lack of choice for consumers.

LSA 2007 addressed these concerns in a number of ways, such as:

1. The creation of the Legal Services Board (**www.legalservicesboard.org.uk**) as an independent supervisory body overseeing the regulation of lawyers in England and Wales through the approved regulators such as the SRA and the Bar Standards Board. Its current business plan for 2019 states: 'our three-year Strategy (2018–21) aims to encourage change in pursuit of a modern and effective legal services sector that works better for consumers, citizens and practitioners'.
2. The transfer of the handling of consumer complaints from the professional bodies to an independent complaints handling organisation, the Office for Legal Complaints, which handles complaints in respect of services offered by all lawyers (i.e. solicitors, barristers, costs lawyers, legal executives, licensed conveyancers, notaries, patent attorneys and trade mark attorneys, registered European lawyers and employees of these businesses).
3. The creation of a statutory framework for the licensing of alternative business structures (ABSs) which enables lawyers to be in partnership, or other business forms, with non-lawyers, and to accept external investment and operate with external ownership.
4. The requirement that professional bodies must separate their regulatory and representative functions.
5. The requirement that all regulators must promote statutory objectives, known as regulatory objectives, and be designated as approved regulators.

4.3 ROLE OF THE LAW SOCIETY

In response to LSA 2007, the Law Society separated its representative and regulatory functions. The Law Society continues with its representative role while the regulatory role has been delegated to the SRA and its Board.

The Law Society represents solicitors in England and Wales. It has a variety of responsibilities: it negotiates with and lobbies the profession's regulators, government and others on behalf of its members; it offers training and advice; it represents the interests of the profession worldwide; and generally seeks to protect and promote solicitors and the solicitors' profession in England and Wales.

The Law Society Group includes the SRA, which is the independent regulator.

4.4 WHAT IS THE SRA?

The Solicitors Regulation Authority (SRA) is part of the Law Society Group and is the independent regulator of solicitors, the majority of law firms in England and Wales, and all those working within such firms. It regulates in the public interest. It deals with all regulatory and disciplinary matters, and sets, monitors and enforces standards for solicitors and the firms it authorises across England and Wales.

Although the Law Society is the approved regulator under LSA 2007, all its regulatory functions are delegated to the SRA, which must comply with the regulatory objectives set out in LSA 2007, s.1. These are shown below, along with the professional principles which are supported by the objectives.

> **1 The regulatory objectives**
>
> (1) In this Act a reference to 'the regulatory objectives' is a reference to the objectives of –
>
> (a) protecting and promoting the public interest;
> (b) supporting the constitutional principle of the rule of law;
> (c) improving access to justice;
> (d) protecting and promoting the interests of consumers;
> (e) promoting competition in the provision of services within subsection (2);
> (f) encouraging an independent, strong, diverse and effective legal profession;
> (g) increasing public understanding of the citizen's legal rights and duties;
> (h) promoting and maintaining adherence to the professional principles.
>
> (2) The services within this subsection are services such as are provided by authorised persons (including services which do not involve the carrying on of activities which are reserved legal activities).
>
> (3) The 'professional principles' are –
>
> (a) that authorised persons should act with independence and integrity,
> (b) that authorised persons should maintain proper standards of work,
> (c) that authorised persons should act in the best interests of their clients,
> (d) that persons who exercise before any court a right of audience, or conduct litigation in relation to proceedings in any court, by virtue of being authorised persons should comply with their duty to the court to act with independence in the interests of justice, and
> (e) that the affairs of clients should be kept confidential.

4.5 THE SRA HANDBOOK

In order to demonstrate adherence to the regulatory objectives, the SRA launched the online SRA Handbook on 6 October 2011. That Handbook, and all its subsequent revisions, is available on the SRA website (**www.sra.org.uk**) and was also published in hard copy by the Law Society.

Following these piecemeal revisions, the SRA decided in 2016 that the time was ripe for a more fundamental review of the 2011 Handbook. There were a number of reasons for this. First and foremost, the SRA decided that the 2011 version was not meeting the regulatory objectives, in particular those dealing with access to justice and promoting competition. It also believed there was huge scope for continued rationalisation and simplification and it wanted to 'future proof' the new rules by pitching the mandatory provisions at a sufficiently high level of generality to remove the need for further piecemeal changes. Finally, it wanted to remove provisions that simply restated the law. Following several consultations, under the strap line 'Looking to the future', the final version of a new Handbook – the SRA Standards and Regulations – was approved by the Legal Services Board (LSB) in October 2018 and 2019 and came into effect on 25 November 2019. It brings wide-ranging changes, which will be reviewed throughout this book.

4.6 WHAT CHANGES DO THE SRA STANDARDS AND REGULATIONS BRING?

The 2019 SRA Standards and Regulations bring many changes, especially to in-house practice. In summary, these are:

- A shortened set of Principles.
- Two Codes of Conduct – one to regulate the activities of SRA-authorised firms and the other which applies to the regulated individual.
- The repeal of the Practice Framework Rules (although some provisions will now appear elsewhere in the Standards and Regulations), including rules 1 and 4 governing in-house practice, to allow solicitors to provide unreserved legal services to the public through businesses which are not regulated under LSA 2007.
- The introduction of 'freelance' solicitors who will be able, subject to conditions, to provide reserved legal activities without being authorised as an entity.
- New Accounts Rules which include a new definition of client money.
- Changes to the assessment of character and suitability.
- Transitional arrangements for the introduction of the Solicitors Qualifying Examination.

The Standards and Regulations 2019 are made up of the sets of rules and regulations listed in Table 4.1 with a commentary on their relevance to in-house practice.

Table 4.1 SRA Standards and Regulations 2019

Rules/requirements, etc.	Brief description	Relevance to in-house solicitors
SRA Principles	The fundamental ethical behaviours required of individuals and firms regulated by the SRA, whether traditional firms or ABSs, and whether working in-house or overseas.	Directly relevant to in-house solicitors.
SRA Code of Conduct for Solicitors, RELs and RFLs	The standards which must be achieved by the individual to ensure ethical and competent practice.	Applies to all practising solicitors, RELs and RFLs, regardless of whether their employer is also regulated or is an entity authorised and regulated by the SRA. There is a separate section dealing with the provision of services to the public which will be relevant to those in-house lawyers employed to provide legal services to the public. It covers client care and complaints handling.
SRA Code of Conduct for Firms	The standards and business controls required of firms that are authorised by the SRA.	Does not apply directly – other than to those whose employer decides to provide services through an ABS. However, the SRA has indicated in guidance that in-house solicitors providing services to the public will need to adopt the systems and procedures expected of authorised firms.
SRA Accounts Rules	Rules designed to ensure that client money is safe.	These now only apply to authorised bodies and their managers and employees. The Code for Individuals prevents those employed in-house from holding client money except in 'prescribed' circumstances. It is anticipated that these circumstances will cover those employed in the not-for-profit sector.

Rules/requirements, etc.	Brief description	Relevance to in-house solicitors
SRA Application, Notice, Review and Appeal Rules	Rules governing applications made to the SRA and reviews and appeals of its decisions.	These apply to all individuals and firms.
SRA Assessment of Character and Suitability Rules	Set out factors to be taken into account for those applying for admission or for restoration to the roll or applying to be an authorised role holder.	Only relevant to those practising solicitors whose employer wishes to become an ABS in order to provide reserved legal services to the public. In those circumstances, they may need to be approved as suitable to be a role holder such as a Compliance Officer for Legal Practice (COLP).
SRA Authorisation of Firms Rules	Set the criteria for firms and individuals seeking authorisation by the SRA.	Not relevant to in-house practice except those whose employer wishes to become an ABS.
SRA Authorisation of Individuals (Amendment) Regulations	Rules and regulations concerning training stages, admission, removal and restoration to the roll, applications for practising certificates, registration as a European or Foreign Lawyer and what authorisation allows authorised individuals to do.	Apply to all in-house solicitors and are closely aligned with the need to consider whether a practising certificate is needed.
SRA Education, Training and Assessment Provider Regulations	These regulations set out the requirements governing organisations which are providing or intending to provide education and training, and the delivery of assessments to those seeking to be admitted as solicitors.	Not directly relevant as they concern the requirements for training providers.
SRA Roll, Registers and Publication Regulations	Sets out the content of the roll and registers the SRA is required to keep about the individuals it regulates.	Will be relevant to all solicitors as it sets out information about them, including any conditions on their practising certificates or findings of the disciplinary tribunal.

Rules/requirements, etc.	Brief description	Relevance to in-house solicitors
SRA Indemnity Insurance Rules	These rules apply to solicitors, registered European lawyers, registered foreign lawyers, and all entities authorised and regulated by the SRA and carrying on private practice in England and Wales. They provide financial protections by ensuring that negligence claims against firms, their managers and employees can be met.	In-house solicitors are not subject to these rules. In-house solicitors who are employed to provide legal services to the public must have insurance but it cannot be with a qualifying insurer under these rules. If an in-house team provides services to clients in circumstances where they will now need to be authorised as an ABS, then the ABS must have professional indemnity insurance in compliance with the SRA Indemnity Insurance Rules.
SRA Indemnity (Enactment) Rules	They continue in force (old Indemnity Rules dealing with historical cover and claims still arising).	Not relevant.
SRA Compensation Fund Rules	Rules regulating the Compensation Fund maintained by the Law Society, and administered by the SRA, for making grants in respect of compensation claims. This means that clients may be compensated if their money has been misappropriated and no other remedies are available to them.	Individual solicitors make a compulsory flat-fee contribution to the Compensation Fund as part of their annual practising certificate application regardless of their type of employment. In-house teams which become ABSs will also be liable to pay a firm-based fee to the Fund. In-house solicitors providing legal services to the public must inform their clients that the Compensation Fund is not available to them.
SRA Statutory Trust Rules	Rules which provide financial protections for clients by requiring that money belonging to clients can be returned to them if the SRA intervenes in a firm.	These rules will not be relevant to in-house solicitors, unless they choose to become an ABS.

Rules/requirements, etc.	Brief description	Relevance to in-house solicitors
SRA Regulatory and Disciplinary Procedure Rules	Rules which govern the procedures for the SRA to discipline regulated individuals, for example by the use of written rebuke, payment of a penalty, etc. and the charges the SRA can make for disciplinary action against an individual.	These rules can be applied to any regulated person including an in-house solicitor.
SRA Overseas and Cross-border Practice Rules	These Rules regulate authorised firms and individuals who practise overseas on a permanent basis; the Cross-border Rules regulate those who engage in cross-border activities within the EU.	These rules will apply to in-house practices overseas.
SRA Financial Services (Scope) Rules	Rules which set the limit of, and conditions for, financial services activities which may be undertaken by law firms which are not authorised by the Financial Conduct Authority (FCA).	These rules regulate private practice activities. In-house solicitors cannot rely on these rules to carry on financial services activities for their employers and clients and need to consider their employer's position under the Financial Services and Markets Act 2000.
SRA Financial Services (Conduct of Business) Rules	Rules which apply when solicitors and others in law firms authorised and regulated by the SRA carry on financial services in accordance with the SRA Financial Services (Scope) Rules 2001. These rules set down requirements about how to carry on such activities.	As above. In-house solicitors carrying on financial services activities need to consider whether their employer needs to be authorised by the FCA and consider compliance requirements in accordance with the FCA Handbook.

Rules/requirements, etc.	Brief description	Relevance to in-house solicitors
SRA Transparency Rules	These set out the costs and other information that firms which undertake certain types of work must give to their clients.	Relevant to solicitors employed in-house who provide legal services to the public, who must inform clients that indemnity insurance under the terms of the Indemnity Rules is not available to them; neither is the Compensation Fund.
SRA Glossary	A glossary of defined terms which are used in the Standards and Regulations.	The Glossary is intended to assist everyone using the Standards and Regulations.

4.7 THE SRA'S STYLE OF REGULATION

The new Standards and Regulations continue the SRA's drive to focus on high-level ethical standards rather than detailed rules. This means increased emphasis on the Principles, which is evidenced by the fact that in most disciplinary proceedings before the Tribunal the SRA alleges, first and foremost, breaches of the relevant Principles. In its Enforcement Strategy published in February 2019 the SRA said that it wanted 'to promote a culture where ethical values and behaviours are embedded'.

The SRA also continues to underline its role as a risk-based regulator with its twice-yearly risk outlook and its risk index and other publications on the subject of risk. The SRA's main concern is the likelihood of high-risk events occurring and the impact that this will have both on the SRA as a regulator and on the public it protects. The risk outlook highlights the key risks and challenges facing solicitors and their firms for the period under review. Most recently, these have covered such subjects as a lack of access to legal services, standards of service, money laundering and information security. Concerns over access to legal services encouraged the SRA to remove the restrictions on in-house practice in order to enable solicitors to provide non-reserved legal services as employees of unregulated entities.

As part of its risk-based approach to regulation, the SRA periodically conducts thematic reviews of certain types of work or issues. These have included looking at how firms deal with the money laundering regulations (their systems and procedures and how effective they are), personal injury work (how clients are obtained, whether there are any payments for referrals and whether these are Legal Aid, Sentencing and Punishment of Offenders Act 2012 (LASPO) compliant) and conveyancing. It is interesting to speculate on whether, and how, the SRA might conduct a thematic review of in-house practice where services are being provided to the public. Undoubtedly, the SRA will want to keep a close eye on how this new area of practice develops but to conduct a review will require cooperation from the employer which might not be forthcoming.

The SRA continues to refine its organisational structure to support its regulatory approach. The SRA's structure, however, still centres on three main departments: authorisation, supervision and enforcement.

4.7.1 Authorisation

The authorisation department deals with applications from both individuals and firms and decides, in respect of the latter, whether it is safe to authorise the entity with or without conditions attached to that authorisation. The SRA Authorisation of Firms Rules require the SRA to approve the prospective managers (partners, directors or members depending on the vehicle used), owners and compliance officers of all firms it authorises. This work is undertaken by the authorisation team, which must have regard to the Assessment of Character and Suitability Rules. The handling of all applications must be done in accordance with the Application, Notice, Review and Appeal Rules.

4.7.2 Supervision

Supervision tends to focus on the firm and how it functions as an entity. There will, however, be action taken where appropriate against individuals who breach the rules. The SRA's supervisory function has been refined and supervision is very much designed to be a proportionate response to the risks posed by both firms and individuals. Firms which are identified as posing a significant risk to the public will have a different supervisory experience, described as relationship management, with the SRA in comparison with those which are deemed to be medium or low impact.

Supervision is the first port of call for reports of problems with firms and individuals. These reports may come from many different sources, including a Compliance Officer for Legal Practice (COLP), a Compliance Officer for Finance and Administration (COFA) and an individual self-reporting or from external agencies, such as the courts or police. They are all assessed and may result in further investigations being conducted. To a certain extent, the supervision team is the sorting house for the SRA. It tries to encourage compliance by working with individuals and firms that have regulatory issues, and attempts to get them on the right track. However, if this approach is unsuccessful, particularly if a firm or individual is uncooperative, then the supervision team also exercises some of the SRA's disciplinary powers to deal with non-compliance. Primarily they will use regulatory settlement agreements under which a firm or individual accepts certain findings of misconduct and agrees a penalty, usually a fine, and to change their behaviour.

4.7.3 Enforcement

The role of the enforcement department has been subject to continuing evaluation. Most of the routine disciplinary investigation work and imposition of sanctions is now done by the supervision department. This means that the enforcement team focuses on the more difficult disciplinary work which tends to result in contested cases before the Solicitors Disciplinary Tribunal (SDT). They will also deal with appeals to the court.

None of this may seem to be of huge relevance to in-house lawyers. However, SRA regulation cannot be ignored or disregarded by any authorised person. This is particularly so now that the SRA has introduced a new Code of Conduct which is applicable specifically to the individuals it regulates, with a separate Code regulating authorised firms. Having said that, it is probably safe to predict that those who work only for their employers and related bodies are less likely to be troubled by the SRA, unless they do something to bring the profession into disrepute such as picking up a criminal conviction.

There also remains the fact that it would only be possible to carry out an in-depth investigation into the activities of an in-house lawyer with the cooperation of the employer and, at present, the SRA has other more pressing issues to grapple with. The position of in-house lawyers working for unauthorised bodies and providing legal services to the public – as is now permitted – will no doubt engage the SRA's interest. How this new form of in-house practice is to be regulated is explored in detail throughout this book.

All in-house lawyers should, however, always have an awareness of regulatory compliance, including what needs to be done and what can go wrong. In addition, in the event that the employer's business becomes an ABS which is authorised and regulated by the SRA, then the SRA's supervisory regime will be applied to that entity, which means it will need to be able to prove that it has effective management and financial and risk management principles in place.

4.8 THE CONSEQUENCES OF A BREACH FOR THE INDIVIDUAL SOLICITOR

The most obvious reason why regulation should not be ignored is because of the disciplinary repercussions.

The SRA explained as long ago as 2011 that its Enforcement Strategy was to:

- create a credible deterrence of behaviours that breach the core principles;
- encourage and facilitate compliance with the core principles and other regulatory requirements;
- control the activities of firms that represent a risk to the public or the core principles; and
- remove those who represent a serious risk to the public.

Again, the focus of this does not seem to be directed at in-house lawyers and there are no explicit references to in-house risks. However, in-house lawyers should not be complacent about their exposure to the SRA's enforcement activities. Reports of potential breaches may reach the SRA from many diverse sources, as illustrated by the high profile case of Alistair Brett, the senior in-house solicitor at the Times Newspapers Limited, who appeared before the Leveson inquiry into the culture, practices and ethics of the British press. As a result of evidence given by him to the inquiry, it became apparent that there were questions to be answered concerning his conduct as a solicitor. The SRA used this evidence to bring a case before the SDT where Brett was found to have acted without integrity and to have allowed the court to be misled. He was suspended from practice for six months. More details on this case appear in **Chapter 5**.

CHAPTER 5

SRA Principles, SRA Code of Conduct for Solicitors, RELs and RFLs and SRA Transparency Rules

5.1 INTRODUCTION

The SRA Principles 2019 and the SRA Code of Conduct for Solicitors, RELs and RFLs 2019 (the Code for Individuals) are the main areas of the SRA Standards and Regulations which are relevant to those practising in-house. They set out the fundamental behaviours required of the individual practising lawyer and govern how lawyers conduct their practice whether in private practice or in-house. All the principles apply to those employed in-house, as do the standards in the Code, although some may not be relevant to many in-house situations, such as those dealing with referrals, introductions and separate businesses.

How the Principles and Code affect in-house practice is dealt with in detail in this chapter. There is also a brief look at:

- the in-house lawyer and their employer as a client of a private practice firm and problems that can arise; and
- the extent to which the SRA is likely to enforce the Code standards in relation to in-house practice.

5.2 SRA PRINCIPLES 2019

The Principles set out the fundamental requirements of a lawyer regulated by the SRA. They preface the SRA Standards and Regulations to make clear that they apply at all times and in all situations, including behaviour outside practice. The Principles should be used to help with the interpretation of all other rules and standards. They go to the root of professionalism and define the values associated with it. They should guide the actions of all those employed in-house in exactly the same way as they apply to those engaged in private practice. Increasingly, when things go wrong the SRA and the Solicitors Disciplinary Tribunal (SDT) will measure behaviour against the Principles, as recent disciplinary decisions attest.

Just because the Code or the Accounts Rules do not expressly cover a situation it does not necessarily mean that it is acceptable to proceed. Reference should always be made to the Principles.

The Principles have been re-worked and there are now just seven principles. Under the 2011 Principles there were ten principles; however, four have been moved into the Codes on the basis that they concern practice management and service standards and cooperation with regulators rather than higher level ethical obligations, and a new principle has been added which requires the lawyer to act with honesty. This is intended to circumvent arguments that had arisen about whether a lack of integrity necessarily implied a lack of honesty, and there are now separate principles requiring both integrity and honesty. The Principles require that you must act:

1. in a way that upholds the constitutional principle of the rule of law, and the proper administration of justice;
2. in a way that upholds public trust and confidence in the solicitors' profession and in the legal services provided by authorised persons;
3. with independence;
4. with honesty;
5. with integrity;
6. in a way that encourages equality, diversity and inclusion; and
7. in the best interests of each client.

Principle 3 dealing with independence can create certain tensions in relation to in-house practice because of the nature of the relationship with the employer client. In private practice it is easier for the lawyer to be totally objective with the client about the parameters of the relationship and what the lawyer can and cannot do. If things go wrong, the lawyer may lose a client but not their job. It is also undoubtedly the case that most employers will respect the need for their lawyers to comply with their regulatory obligations and to respect their independence to be able to decide what they can and cannot do. However, there are some employers that will push the boundaries and in-house lawyers must be quite clear about what they cannot do, particularly in relation to their duty to the court. The new form of in-house practice where solicitors are permitted to act for the public through unauthorised bodies may well see the rise of tensions between employer and lawyer which may threaten the lawyer's independence. The commercial imperative may well clash with the lawyer's ethical obligations. There is more on this issue in **Chapter 7**.

Where two or more principles come into conflict, those that take precedence are those which best serve the wider public interest such as the rule of law and public confidence in the solicitors' profession and legal services. These would require that, as a lawyer, you must inform your client if your duties to the court outweigh your obligations to your client. This is most likely to arise if your client, or the individual representing your client, wants to mislead the court for their own benefit or for the benefit of the company employer. This has further amplification in the Code for Individuals, section 2, dealing with the lawyer's duties to the court (see **5.5.2** below).

Finally, in-house lawyers should be aware that the SRA is increasingly using the Principles to bring disciplinary proceedings for conduct which arises outside legal practice. This can include inappropriate sexual conduct and minor criminal convictions such as drink driving.

5.3 TWO SRA CODES OF CONDUCT – ONE FOR INDIVIDUALS, THE OTHER FOR FIRMS

One of the major changes brought in by the new SRA Standards and Regulations is the introduction of two Codes of Conduct, which are the:

- SRA Code of Conduct for Solicitors, RELs and RFLs, which has application to authorised individuals (the Code for Individuals); and the
- SRA Code of Conduct for Firms, which has application to SRA-authorised firms (the Code for Firms).

In its preamble to the Code for Individuals, the SRA says that it 'describes the standards of professionalism that we, the SRA, and the public expect of individuals (solicitors, registered European lawyers and registered foreign lawyers) authorised by us to provide legal services'. It applies in its entirety to lawyers working in-house and, unlike the previous Code, does not seek to identify sections that have application specifically to in-house practice, while disapplying others. Having said that, the extent to which different obligations apply will be determined by the nature of in-house practice in which the lawyer is employed. For example, paragraphs 5.1–5.3 in the Code ('Referrals, introductions and separate businesses') is very unlikely to have application to the more traditional forms of in-house practice where services are provided exclusively to the employer. However, it may well have application to the newer forms of practice where services are provided to the public. Worthy of mention is the fact that there is a section (covering paragraphs 8.1, 8.2–8.5 and 8.6–8.11) which applies solely to those providing services to the public, and this will be important to those who are employed in-house to act for the public.

The Code for Firms does not apply to in-house practice. Its focus is on business controls and the need for systems and procedures to enable firms to be well managed so that they can provide a competent and ethical service to clients. However, where in-house lawyers offer services to the public, guidance issued by the SRA on this new form of practice takes the view that to meet the standards in the Code for Individuals, there will need to be systems in place to deal with issues like conflicts of interest and protecting client confidentiality. Without these systems, it may prove difficult to demonstrate compliance with these and other duties set out in the Code for Individuals. For this reason, those who provide legal services to the public as part of their employment would be advised to have some regard to the Code for Firms.

5.4 THE USE OF STANDARDS IN THE NEW CODES

The emphasis in both 2019 Codes is on achieving standards, rather than meeting outcomes as required by the 2011 Code. The preamble to the Code for Individuals says that they 'comprise a framework for ethical and competent practice which applies irrespective of your role or the environment or organisation in which you work'. It is difficult to envisage that the change from outcomes to standards makes any significant difference, as both impose mandatory requirements. It is possible that the SRA wanted to make the requirements of the new Codes appear to have a harder edge and they are largely phrased in terms of what you must and must not do. They continue to be pitched at a high level of generality and provide even greater flexibility for lawyers and firms to make their own decisions about the sort of information they need to give their clients and the relationship they have with them. This continues to mean that those who act for sophisticated users of legal services have the ability to deal with their clients in a way which is different from the approach needed for those who act for individuals who rarely use legal services. The use of high level standards is also much more appropriate to in-house practice than the more detailed requirements which, in the past, have tended to reflect the needs of private practice.

This continued greater flexibility places responsibility on individuals and firms to demonstrate how they have met the standards and to show what steps they have taken to identify and deal with risks of non-compliance. Those in private practice, and also those employed by organisations such as law centres and unauthorised bodies, are likely to demonstrate compliance primarily through their client care letters and terms of business, and through information provided on their websites.

For most lawyers working in-house, the use of formal terms of business will not be an option and the relationship with the client, usually the employer, will be governed by their contract of employment. Nonetheless, this does not negate the fact that lawyers should obtain clear instructions from their employers about all aspects of the work undertaken and have a proper dialogue over how it is to be achieved. Should there be a dispute over whether a lawyer has met the standards, documented evidence of their instructions and how they were met will assist the lawyer in exactly the same way as in private practice.

For all lawyers, the emphasis is very much on demonstrating ethical conduct, with the scene being set in section 1 of the Codes entitled 'Maintaining trust and acting fairly'.

From time to time, the employer/employee relationship may create some tensions on an individual's ability to meet the standards. This may be, for example, because the employer wants an employee to take on legal work in a field that the individual does not feel they have the competence to deal with. Any refusal to carry out that work may have adverse consequences for their future employment. However, the employee is under an obligation to meet a standard which requires that 'you ensure that the service you provide to clients is competent …'. The only way for individuals to deal with this type of situation may be to make clear in writing their concern about their lack of ability to undertake the work and suggesting that, perhaps, external expertise should be used, where necessary, to ensure the work is not compromised.

Finally, the standards in the 2019 Codes are not accompanied by indicative behaviours, which were a feature of the 2011 Code. The SRA always had concerns that the indicative behaviours might be viewed as creating restrictions on the flexibility of the outcomes. In other words, they would be seen as the only way of achieving compliance and effectively be viewed as mandatory. In short, the SRA believes that solicitors should be encouraged to think for themselves about ethical compliance and look less for prompts. Solicitors will, therefore, need to make their own decisions about how they achieve the standards. This will be easier in relation to those that are more detailed, such as those dealing with conflicts of interest and the duty of confidentiality. In place of the indicative behaviours, toolkits and extensive guidance to deal with specific issues, partly based around case studies, are now being published on the SRA's website. Three sets of guidance are provided specifically for the new form of practice where in-house lawyers provide legal services to the public. The first is aimed at the lawyers, the second at their employers, and the third looks specifically at dealing with conflicts of interest and the duty of confidentiality, and includes case studies. All this will be considered in more detail in **Chapter 7**.

These and other changes introduced by the 2019 Codes will be examined in more depth as the different sections of the Code for Individuals are analysed in this chapter.

5.5 CONTENT AND STRUCTURE OF THE CODE FOR INDIVIDUALS

The 2019 Code has been pared back, and is now much more high level than the 2011 Code. It has been reduced to just seven pages. The preamble says:

> You must exercise your judgement in applying these standards to the situations you are in and deciding on a course of action, bearing in mind your role and responsibilities, areas of practice and the nature of your clients (which in an in house context will generally include your employer and may include other persons or groups within or outside your employer organisation).

It does not impose any new obligations, and so does not require individuals to change their behaviours and systems to be compliant. The material has been re-ordered, which means that initially the task which faces readers is to discover where different obligations have gone – and even if they still exist. References to compliance with legislation have gone but, in the preamble, the SRA makes clear that it has a legal obligation to monitor and enforce requirements relating to referral fees under the Legal Aid, Sentencing and Punishment of Offenders Act 2012 and provisions relating to anti-money laundering (AML) and counter-terrorism financing.

The material is now broken down into the following rules which will be looked at in detail:

1. Maintaining trust and acting fairly.
2. Dispute resolution and proceedings before courts, tribunals and inquiries.
3. Service and competence.
4. Client money and assets.
5. Business requirements.
6. Conflict, confidentiality and disclosure.
7. Cooperation and accountability.
8. Providing services to the public or a section of the public.

5.5.1 Maintaining trust and acting fairly

Section 1 ('Maintaining trust and acting fairly') is very much underpinned by the principle requiring you to act with integrity. Also relevant is principle 6 requiring you to act in a way that 'encourages equality, diversity and inclusion'. Generally, this represents a massive contraction of two sections in the previous Code covering 'Equality and diversity' and 'Relations with third parties'. Although the SRA does not encourage this, it is probably a good idea to refer to a copy of the 2011 Code of Conduct as it sets out in its outcomes and indicative behaviours ways of avoiding discrimination and demonstrating how you have done so. The new Code sets out the following obligations:

1.1 not unfairly discriminating 'by allowing your personal views to affect your relationships and the way in which you provide your services';
1.2 not abusing your position 'by taking unfair advantage of *clients* and others';
1.3 performing 'all *undertakings* given by you, and [doing] so within an agreed timescale or if no timescale has been agreed then within a reasonable amount of time';
1.4 not misleading 'your *clients*, the *court* or others either by your own acts or omissions or allowing or being complicit in the acts or omissions of others (including your *client*)'.

The Code for Individuals, paragraph 1.1, applies generally to all forms of practice, including in-house, and it will, in all probability, be embraced by most employers which are likely to have policies covering discrimination, diversity and inclusion. It specifically refers to your 'personal views' not influencing 'your relationships' and the services you provide. Although no longer expressly mentioned in the Code, compliance with the law concerning discrimination is still essential. The backdrop to any form of discrimination are the protected characteristics set out in the Equality Act 2010, which are:

- age;
- disability;
- gender reassignment;
- marriage and civil partnership;
- pregnancy and maternity;
- race;
- religion or belief;
- sex; and
- sexual orientation.

There is limited evidence of the SRA pursuing discrimination cases, although in 2017 the case of *SRA* v. *Mahmood* (SDT 11625/2017) resulted in a finding of discrimination where a solicitor had posted anti-Zionist comments on Facebook which were considered discriminatory against a colleague.

Paragraph 1.2 also has obvious application to in-house practice, as fair dealing with people, whether clients or others, is fundamental to the ethical standards expected of lawyers. It has particular application to court proceedings where it links to principle 1 (upholding the rule of law and proper administration of justice). Principle 2 is also relevant, as fair dealing with others helps uphold public trust in the solicitors' profession and the legal services provided by it.

Paragraph 1.3 deals with undertakings which may have limited use for in-house work. They might, however, be used more frequently by in-house lawyers providing services to the public under the new rule relaxations. Complying with undertakings is treated very seriously by the SRA as it is a manifestation of acting honestly and with integrity. Failure to comply is likely to lead to disciplinary sanctions. The SRA Glossary contains the definition of an undertaking:

> a statement, given orally or in writing, whether or not it includes the word 'undertake' or 'undertaking', to someone who reasonably places reliance on it, that you or a third party will do something or cause something to be done, or refrain from doing something.

The reference to you or 'a third party' doing something pursuant to an undertaking is interesting as it does not appear in the previous definition of an undertaking. It raises the possibility that if a lawyer says that their employer will do something, the lawyer will be held liable if the employer then fails to do what was promised. Statements about what your employer will do should, therefore, only be made with caution. Having said that, guidance given in the past has always emphasised that solicitors should never promise to do something that was outside their control.

Paragraph 1.4 is a high level statement, concerning the requirement not to mislead people and the courts, which again is underpinned by the requirements of honesty and integrity set out in the Principles. More detail about the solicitor's relationship with the court appears in section 2.

5.5.2 Dispute resolution and proceedings before courts, tribunals and inquiries

Section 2 ('Dispute resolution and proceedings before courts, tribunals and inquiries') deals with how lawyers must behave in contentious matters, and the concepts are not new. Again, this has been pruned in comparison with the outcomes in the previous Code. The requirements are:

2.1 You do not misuse or tamper with evidence or attempt to do so.
2.2 You do not seek to influence the substance of evidence, including generating false evidence or persuading witnesses to change their evidence.
2.3 You do not provide or offer to provide any benefit to witnesses dependent upon the nature of their evidence or the outcome of the case.
2.4 You only make assertions or put forward statements, representations or submissions to the *court* or others which are properly arguable.
2.5 You do not place yourself in contempt of *court*, and you comply with *court* orders which place obligations on you.
2.6 You do not waste the *court's* time.
2.7 You draw the *court's* attention to relevant cases and statutory provisions, or procedural irregularities of which you are aware, and which are likely to have a material effect on the outcome of the proceedings.

All these obligations will apply to all in-house lawyers who conduct litigation or appear as advocates. The language is clear and underpins principle 1, which requires adherence to the rule of law and acting in a way that upholds the proper administration of justice. This is a fundamental obligation placed on solicitors as officers of the court.

Interestingly, an outcome which was introduced in the previous Code has been dropped. This was an obligation to inform clients of circumstances in which your duties to the court outweigh your duties to the client. It is possible that the SRA now views this as being implied by principle 1 (upholding the rule of law) but it should not be assumed that the former obligation no longer applies.

5.5.3 Service and competence

Section 3 ('Service and competence') is very much a manifestation of principle 7 (acting in the best interests of clients). As an in-house lawyer, the client is often your employer and the service expected of you may be contained substantially in your employment contract. What is competent will be largely determined by your employer. This will have variable application to in-house practice:

3.1 You only act for *clients* on instructions from the *client*, or from someone properly authorised to provide instructions on their behalf. If you have reason to suspect that the instructions do not represent your *client's* wishes, you do not act unless you have satisfied yourself that they do. However, in circumstances where you have legal authority to act notwithstanding that it is not possible to obtain or ascertain the instructions of your *client*, then you are subject to the overriding obligation to protect your *client's* best interests.

3.2 You ensure that the service you provide to *clients* is competent and delivered in a timely manner.

3.3 You maintain your competence to carry out your role and keep your professional knowledge and skills up to date.

3.4 You consider and take account of your *client's* attributes, needs and circumstances.

3.5 Where you supervise or manage others providing legal services:

(a) you remain accountable for the work carried out through them; and
(b) you effectively supervise work being done for *clients*.

3.6 You ensure that the individuals you manage are competent to carry out their role, and keep their professional knowledge and skills, as well as understanding of their legal, ethical and regulatory obligations, up to date.

The need for a service to be competent and the tensions that that may create for those employed in-house was considered above in **5.4**.

The need to keep professional knowledge and skills up to date has universal application and ties in with the SRA's continuing competency regime. This requires solicitors to review their learning and development needs at least annually and to keep a record of that review and the action taken to address identified needs. This moves away from the previous formulaic approach to continuing professional development and the obligation to complete a specified number of hours of training, to a more sensible approach which places the responsibility on individuals to review their personal training requirements. For those working in-house it is likely that their annual review of training needs as a lawyer will be conducted in conjunction with their employer or line manager, probably as part of an appraisal process. This should help with record-keeping, which is important to evidence compliance.

Additionally, these requirements affect those who have supervisory roles within in-house legal departments and place clear responsibility on them to manage their team effectively. Where lawyers providing legal services to the public are employed by unauthorised bodies, it will be very important for their contract of employment to be clear as to exactly whom they are responsible for supervising, particularly where other services are offered alongside legal services.

5.5.4 Client money and assets

Section 4 ('Client money and assets') concern the safeguarding of money and assets 'entrusted to you by clients and others'. Paragraph 4.3 prevents you, as a solicitor, from holding client money unless you work in an authorised firm or an organisation of a kind 'prescribed' by the SRA. Guidance issued by the SRA for the not-for-profit sector makes clear that in-house lawyers working in that sector can hold client money in their own name on 'the terms prescribed'. These terms are set out in an SRA 'Statement of the prescribed organisations and terms under which solicitors, RELs and RFLs are allowed to hold client money in their own name'. The prescribed terms to a large extent mirror the Accounts Rules which apply to regulated firms. More detail appears in **Chapter 6**.

5.5.5 Referrals, introductions and separate businesses

Paragraphs 5.1 to 5.3 ('Referrals, introductions and separate businesses') cover fee sharing, referral fees and separate businesses. It is unlikely to have application to most in-house practice where work is done for the employer and related entities or individuals. However, for those employed by unauthorised bodies providing legal services to the public, this could be important where referrals are received from, or made to, third parties in respect of the legal work. These paragraphs refer to referrals made 'by you' and introductions of business 'to you' which raises an interesting debate about whether referrals and introductions made to and by your employer are 'by you' or 'to you' and therefore whether the standard applies. However, both the SRA and the Law Society in their guidance for those working in this form of in-house practice seem clear that it will always apply.

Where a payment is made for any referral of business you make or any introduction you receive or in respect of any fee sharing arrangement, paragraph 5.1 requires the following:

(a) *clients* are informed of any financial or other interest which you or your business or employer has in referring the *client* to another *person* or which an introducer has in referring the *client* to you;
(b) *clients* are informed of any fee-sharing arrangement that is relevant to their matter;
(c) the fee sharing agreement is in writing;
(d) [payments are not allowed to be made or received in respect of clients who are the subject of criminal proceedings – this will be irrelevant to in-house practice as it is a reserved activity]; and
(e) any *client* referred by an introducer has not been acquired in a way which would breach the *SRA's regulatory arrangements* if the person acquiring the client was regulated by the *SRA*.

Paragraph 5.2 states that 'Where it appears to the *SRA* that you have received a *referral fee* the payment will be treated as a *referral fee* unless you show that the payment was not made as such'. The definition of 'referral fee' in the SRA Glossary says it means 'a referral fee as defined in section 57(7) of the Legal Aid, Sentencing and Punishment of Offenders Act 2012'. Paragraph 5.2 is, therefore, referring to the specific situation where the referral fee is of 'prescribed legal business', which at present means personal injury work. It is unlikely to affect any in-house lawyer as any services provided to the public must be non-reserved.

Paragraph 5.3 deals with separate businesses and has application to the situation where clients are referred between an authorised firm and a business that is not a body authorised to provide legal services. The term 'separate business' is defined in the SRA Glossary and means:

a separate business

(a) which you own;
(b) which you are owned by;
(c) where you actively participate in the provision of its services, including where you have any direct control over the business or any indirect control over the business through another person; or

(d) which you are connected with,

and which is not an authorised body, an authorised non-SRA firm, or an overseas practice.

Paragraph 5.3 will be relevant to in-house solicitors providing legal services to the public if they are employed by a separate business. This may, for example, be where an SRA-authorised firm decides to offer some of its non-reserved legal services through a separate business and employ a solicitor in that business. In those circumstances, paragraph 5.3 must be complied with and, although this should be the responsibility of the referring firm, the in-house solicitor dealing with the referred work should check that it has been complied with. The standard requires that the client gives informed consent to the referral or, where part of a matter is referred, to that part being referred.

5.5.6 Conflict, confidentiality and disclosure

In relation to conflicts of interest, as with the duties of confidentiality and disclosure, the standard is intended to align with the common law obligations which arise from the fiduciary nature of the relationship between solicitor and client. Failure to comply with the standard, therefore, may also give rise to a breach of common law duties. For most traditional in-house lawyers who provide services largely limited to their employer, the conflict standard will only apply in very limited situations, as they will rarely represent two or more clients. For those employed to provide services to the public, compliance with the standard is high risk and compliance should be achieved by implementing the systems and procedures required of those working in authorised firms and subject to the Code for Firms.

The underpinning principle in all conflict of interest situations is that you must 'act in the best interests of each client'. The definition of a 'conflict of interest' is drafted around this principle and is set out in the SRA Glossary 2019. The definition says a conflict of interest 'means a situation where your separate duties to act in the best interests of two or more clients in relation to the same or a related matters conflict'. The definition of 'own interest conflict' is slightly longer and states that it is 'any situation where your duty to act in the best interests of any client in relation to a matter conflicts, or there is a significant risk that it may conflict, with your own interests in relation to that or a related matter'.

The inclusion of 'related matters' in the client conflict of interest definition reflects the decision of the Court of Appeal in *Marks & Spencer Group Plc and another* v. *Freshfields Bruckhaus Deringer* [2004] EWCA Civ 741. This 2004 decision remains the leading authority on conflict involving related matters. The facts, very briefly, are that the firm involved routinely acted for Marks and Spencer and at the time in question was in the process of re-negotiating on Marks and Spencer's behalf a major contract for one of its clothing brands. It then accepted instructions from a client wishing to make a hostile takeover bid for the company. Marks and Spencer successfully applied for an injunction. The court found that the work the firm was doing for the company was likely to have an impact on its share price. The value of the shares was important in any takeover bid. Although the instructions for the two clients did not concern the same matter, the court decided that they had to be related as what the firm was doing for one client would clearly impact on the other. There was, therefore, a conflict and because of this, the firm could not remedy the situation by the use of information barriers.

Paragraphs 6.1 to 6.2 ('Conflict of interests') say:

> 6.1 You do not act if there is an *own interest conflict* or a significant risk of such a conflict.
>
> 6.2 You do not act in relation to a matter or particular aspect of it if you have a *conflict of interest* or a significant risk of such a conflict in relation to that matter or aspect of it, unless:
>
> (a) the *clients* have a *substantially common interest* in relation to the matter or the aspect of it, as appropriate; or
>
> (b) the *clients* are *competing for the same objective*,
>
> and the conditions below are met, namely that:
>
> (i) all the *clients* have given informed consent, given or evidenced in writing, to you acting;
>
> (ii) where appropriate, you put in place effective safeguards to protect your *clients'* confidential information; and
>
> (iii) you are satisfied it is reasonable for you to act for all the *clients*.

Own interest conflict

In-house lawyers who act solely for their employer will only need to be concerned with paragraph 6.1. If any situation should arise where an 'own interest conflict' becomes apparent then the individual concerned must decline the work and ensure that another member of the legal team acts or, if this is not possible, that an external lawyer is instructed. The reasons will have to be explained to the employer. Deciding when it is not possible to act will not always be easy as some employers may be unsympathetic to a lawyer's sensitivities.

There may be situations where the employer's instructions would have an adverse effect on the in-house lawyer but it may, nonetheless, be appropriate to act. This can occur where the in-house lawyer is asked to advise on employment situations that could affect the lawyer personally. To give one example, an in-house lawyer may receive instructions to amend the company's employee share scheme, and the new arrangements are less favourable to the lawyer as an employee. If the lawyer is simply giving effect to the instructions or advising how this could be done legally then it is unlikely that this could give rise to a conflict. The employer has made the decision to make the change and the lawyer is not being asked to influence the employer's decision making.

In any situation where in-house lawyers are asked to advise or act where their own employment interests could be affected, they must always consider whether this is in any way likely to affect their ability to advise and act independently and impartially. It will often be very much a judgment call for the individual concerned.

It will, of course, also be a situation in which the 'conflict', real or otherwise, is not concealed from the employer, in that the employer will know that the lawyer's personal interests are affected. The bottom line for the lawyer will be: can you put your own interests aside or is your position affected to the extent that this is not possible?

Client conflict

Paragraph 6.2 provides a general prohibition on acting where there is a 'client conflict' or a significant risk that one will arise. This type of conflict is likely to have a very different impact on those who act mainly for an employer and those who act for the public.

For those who act mainly for an employer, it might arise in situations where they are also asked to act for another employee. Scenarios could include:

- acting for the employer, the director of the HR department and a fellow employee manager in defending a discrimination case brought against all three; or
- acting for a driver employed by the employer in relation to an assault by a member of the public on the driver when carrying out their employment duties.

In the former situation the lawyer is acting for the employer as well as the employees so there is increased potential for conflict. The employer is likely to be keen to use its in-house lawyer as this will be more cost effective and less disruptive than paying for its employees to have independent advice. In theory, the interests of all are the same if the allegations are being denied and the evidence appears to support that denial. However, the danger is that other evidence may come to light which could indicate that one or both of the employees did discriminate. It may still be acceptable to act for all three but the risk of conflict could increase if it was likely that the employer would want to bring disciplinary action against the employees if the defence failed. The lawyer would have to weigh up whether it will be possible to act in the employees' best interests as well as those of the employer. Issues to consider might be whether one or both of the employees felt unable to give full instructions to the lawyer or discuss their position openly because of the lawyer's duties to the employer.

In the latter situation, the lawyer is only acting for the employee so this is not a conflict in the true sense but it is complicated by the fact that the lawyer owes ongoing duties to the employer. It could be, for example, that the employee was on a 'frolic of his own' and was drinking in a pub instead of working and this was when the assault occurred. The lawyer would have to make it clear at the outset that they could not act if the employee wanted to say something that they did not want the employer to know about.

In the in-house situation there is always likely to be an imbalance in the position of employer and employee and this needs to be kept under review when acting for both. In relation to the possible situations of conflict described above it is prudent to keep a record of any decision-making process about whether it was appropriate to act for employer and employee(s).

Where an in-house lawyer is employed to act for the public, the situation is very much akin to that of private practice. The SRA has issued guidance on conflicts of interest with case studies which should be referred to for further help. Although not covered by the Code for Individuals, there should always be systems and procedures in place, as is required of those in private practice, to identity conflicts and to explain how they should be dealt with. Reference to the Code for Firms is, therefore, appropriate. This Code has the following relevant requirements:

> 2.1 You have effective governance structures, arrangements, systems and controls in place that ensure:
>
> (a) you comply with all the *SRA's regulatory arrangements*, as well as with other regulatory and legislative requirements which apply to you; . . .
>
> 2.2 You keep and maintain records to demonstrate compliance with your obligations under the *SRA's regulatory arrangements*.

Exceptions where you may act where there is conflict

There are two exceptions which permit individuals/firms to act where there is a conflict and they are set out above (see paragraph 6.2). Only one is ever likely to have relevance to in-house practice, as the other is only intended to be applicable to large private practice firms dealing with sophisticated clients. The exception which may be relevant covers situations where two or more clients have a substantially common interest but there is peripheral conflict which can be managed without the need for the clients to receive independent advice elsewhere. The required safeguards which would allow you to act are as follows:

- all the clients must give informed consent which must be given or evidenced in writing;
- where appropriate, effective safeguards must be put in place to protect clients' confidential information; and
- you must be satisfied it is reasonable to act.

The situations where this exception could be used are likely to be rare in relation to in-house practice. It is very unlikely it would be appropriate for situations where the lawyer is acting for both the employer and employee because of the unequal bargaining position between them which might make it difficult to demonstrate that 'it is reasonable to act'. It might, however, be appropriate for a joint venture between, for example, a local authority and another body. If a decision was taken to use this exception the situation would need to be kept under review to ensure that the minor, or peripheral, conflict did not escalate to the point where it was not possible to represent the best interests of both or all clients. If it did, the lawyer would have to cease acting for all clients except the employer.

For those employed by unauthorised bodies and acting for the public, there may be many situations where the exception might be relevant. It could be applicable, for example, where individuals are being advised on the setting up of a small business. They may agree on all the major aspects of what they want to achieve but there could be minor differences to be resolved, where one or more of them might want separate advice. In giving this advice, great care must be taken to ensure that this does not prejudice any of the others involved and that the differences can be resolved. If the situation becomes untenable, one or all of the individuals will need to be advised by another firm or company to resolve the disputed issues.

Confidentiality and disclosure

Paragraphs 6.3 to 6.5 ('Confidentiality and disclosure') say:

> 6.3 You keep the affairs of current and former *clients* confidential unless disclosure is required or permitted by law or the *client* consents.
>
> 6.4 Where you are acting for a *client* on a matter, you make the *client* aware of all the information material to the matter of which you have knowledge, except when:
>
> (a) the disclosure of the information is prohibited by legal restrictions imposed in the interests of national security or the prevention of crime;
> (b) your *client* gives informed consent, given or evidenced in writing, to the information not being disclosed to them;
> (c) you have reason to believe that serious physical or mental injury will be caused to your *client* or another if the information is disclosed; or
> (d) the information is contained in a privileged document that you have knowledge of only because it was mistakenly disclosed.
>
> 6.5 You do not act for a *client* in a matter where that *client* has an interest adverse to the interest of another current or former *client* of you or your business or employer, for whom you or your business or employer holds confidential information which is material to that matter, unless:
>
> (a) effective measures have been taken which result in there being no real risk of disclosure of the confidential information; or
> (b) the current or former *client* whose information you or your business or employer holds has given informed consent, given or evidenced in writing, to you acting, including to any measures taken to protect their information.

Ensuring client confidentiality is a key behaviour that is expected of all lawyers, whether working in private practice or in-house. The SRA continues to flag up the importance of making sure that clients' confidential information is secure, particularly with the rise of cyber crime and the risk that this represents for lawyers. Significant quantities of client information are now stored electronically, including cloud storage, and this requires that anti-malware software must be used, maintained and updated. Those employed in a traditional in-house role are likely to have an employer who controls the company's IT systems and its security. However, for lawyers employed to provide services to the public, the onus will be much more on them to take responsibility for ensuring that client information is protected. If there is a breach, they will be held responsible by the SRA.

There also remain the more conventional risks of conversations between lawyers outside the office being overheard or of client documents being left unsecured in a car, on public transport or in any other public place such as a court. Lawyers working in a supervisory role in-house must make sure that all those working under their supervision are fully aware of the dangers of a breach of client confidentiality. Those employed to provide services to the public should, in particular, make sure there are systems and procedures in place which protect confidential information.

Paragraph 6.5 is unlikely to have relevance to most in-house roles. It may, however, be relevant to those employees of unauthorised bodies acting for the public and it seems to have been drafted with this in mind as it refers to clients of you or 'your business or employer'. It concerns the protection of client confidential information where this is particularly at risk because information is held for one client which is material to another client and the interests of these clients are adverse. This is where the matters of the clients are unrelated. (If the matters were the same, or related, there would be a conflict of interests and it would not be possible to act for both.) The starting point is that in these circumstances you cannot act.

There is, however, a possible workaround. Paragraph 6.5 allows the option of putting 'effective measures' in place to protect the information that is at risk through disclosure (whether inadvertently or otherwise). 'Effective measures' means putting in place an effective information barrier which prevents the confidential information of a client leaking from inside the barrier to reach those acting for the other client, or clients, to whom it would be material. As an alternative, it permits the lawyer to act in this situation with the client's informed consent in writing or evidenced in writing.

Acting under this exception should only be done with extreme caution. First, it is important to bear in mind the principle which requires you to act in each client's best interests. Things to consider before using this exception would include whether it is appropriate to ask a particular client to consent to the use of an information barrier. Generally, only more sophisticated clients will fully appreciate the risks of your acting in these circumstances. Furthermore, most organisations do not have the ability to create an effective information barrier that can guarantee the complete electronic and physical separation of two or more clients' matters.

5.5.7 Cooperation and accountability

Section 7 ('Cooperation and accountability') opens with a requirement in paragraph 7.1 that you to keep up to date with legal and regulatory obligations that affect you. This means keeping abreast of the SRA's rules and regulations and the law that affects the work you do, such as the anti-money laundering requirements and the General Data Protection Regulation. Most of the other requirements in this paragraph relate to keeping the SRA informed of certain events that affect you and the requirement to cooperate with the SRA and other regulators in relation to their enquiries. It is integral to the SRA's obligation to protect the public that any information and documents it requests are provided promptly so that it can form a view about any apparent risks. The SRA will take action where solicitors fail to cooperate and a number of cases that have reached the SDT testify to this. Those who work in-house and provide services to the public need to be aware that the SRA has statutory powers under the Solicitors Act 1974 to formally request documents and information in exactly the same way as if they were employed in private practice.

Paragraph 7.12 will have no application to in-house practice as it refers to making reports to a Compliance Officer for Legal Practice (COLP) and a Compliance Officer for Finance and Administration (COFA), roles only required of SRA-authorised firms.

The requirements are otherwise self-explanatory:

7.1 You keep up to date with and follow the law and regulation governing the way you work.

7.2 You are able to justify your decisions and actions in order to demonstrate compliance with your obligations under the *SRA's regulatory arrangements*.

7.3 You cooperate with the *SRA*, other regulators, ombudsmen, and those bodies with a role overseeing and supervising the delivery of, or investigating concerns in relation to, legal services.

7.4 You respond promptly to the *SRA* and:

(a) provide full and accurate explanations, information and documents in response to any request or requirement; and

(b) ensure that relevant information that is held by you, or third parties carrying out functions on your behalf which are critical to the delivery of your legal services, is available for inspection by the *SRA*.

7.5 You do not attempt to prevent anyone from providing information to the *SRA* or any other body exercising regulatory, supervisory, investigatory or prosecutor functions in the public interest.

7.6 You notify the *SRA* promptly if:

(a) you become subject to any criminal charge, conviction or caution subject to the Rehabilitation of Offenders Act 1974;

(b) a *relevant insolvency event* occurs in relation to you; or

(c) if you become aware:

(i) of any material changes to information previously provided to the *SRA*, by you or on your behalf, about you or your practice, including any change to information recorded in the *register*; and

(ii) that information provided to the *SRA*, by you or on your behalf, about you or your practice is or may be false, misleading, incomplete or inaccurate.

7.7 You report promptly to the *SRA*, or another *approved regulator*, as appropriate, of any serious breach of their *regulatory arrangements* by any *person* regulated by them (including you).

7.8 Notwithstanding paragraph 7.7, you inform the *SRA* promptly of any facts or matters that you reasonably believe should be brought to its attention in order that it may investigate whether a serious breach of its *regulatory arrangements* has occurred or otherwise exercise its regulatory powers.

7.9 You do not subject any *person* to detrimental treatment for making or proposing to make a report or providing or proposing to provide information based on a reasonably held belief under paragraph 7.7 or 7.8 above, or paragraph 3.9, 3.10, 9.1(d) or (e) or 9.2(b) or (c) of the SRA Code of Conduct for Firms, irrespective of whether the *SRA* or another approved regulator subsequently investigates or takes any action in relation to the facts or matters in question.

7.10 You act promptly to take any remedial action requested by the *SRA*. If requested to do so by the *SRA* you investigate whether there have been any serious breaches that should be reported to the *SRA*.

7.11 You are honest and open with *clients* if things go wrong, and if a *client* suffers loss or harm as a result you put matters right (if possible) and explain fully and promptly what has happened and the likely impact. If requested to do so by the *SRA* you investigate whether anyone may have a claim against you, provide the *SRA* with a report on the outcome of your investigation, and notify relevant persons that they may have such a claim, accordingly.

7.12 Any obligation under this section or otherwise to notify, or provide information to, the SRA will be satisfied if you provide information to your firm's *COLP* or *COFA*, as and where appropriate, on the understanding that they will do so.

5.5.8 Providing services to the public or a section of the public

The provisions in paragraphs 8.1 to 8.11 concerning client care do not apply to in-house lawyers who provide services for their employer and related bodies. They do, however, apply to lawyers employed in the not-for-profit sector and by unauthorised bodies providing non-reserved legal services to the public. While section 3 deals with the more general duties owed to clients of service and competence, paragraphs 8.1 to 8.11 take a more detailed look at the following specific areas of the client relationship:

- client identification;
- complaints handling; and
- client information and publicity.

The following obligations exist:

Client identification

8.1 You identify who you are acting for in relation to any matter.

Complaints handling

8.2 You ensure that, as appropriate in the circumstances, you either establish and maintain, or participate in, a procedure for handling complaints in relation to the legal services you provide.

8.3 You ensure that *clients* are informed in writing at the time of engagement about:

(a) their right to complain to you about your services and your charges;
(b) how a complaint can be made and to whom; and
(c) any right they have to make a complaint to the *Legal Ombudsman* and when they can make any such complaint.

8.4 You ensure that when *clients* have made a complaint to you, if this has not been resolved to the *client's* satisfaction within 8 weeks following the making of a complaint they are informed, in writing:

(a) of any right they have to complain to the *Legal Ombudsman*, the time frame for doing so and full details of how to contact the *Legal Ombudsman*; and

(b) if a complaint has been brought and your complaints procedure has been exhausted:

(i) that you cannot settle the complaint;

(ii) of the name and website address of an alternative dispute resolution (ADR) approved body which would be competent to deal with the complaint; and

(iii) whether you agree to use the scheme operated by that body.

8.5 You ensure that complaints are dealt with promptly, fairly, and free of charge.

Client information and publicity

8.6 You give *clients* information in a way they can understand. You ensure they are in a position to make informed decisions about the services they need, how their matter will be handled and the options available to them.

8.7 You ensure that *clients* receive the best possible information about how their matter will be priced and, both at the time of engagement and when appropriate as their matter progresses, about the likely overall cost of the matter and any costs incurred.

8.8 You ensure that any *publicity* in relation to your practice is accurate and not misleading, including that relating to your charges and the circumstances in which *interest* is payable by or to *clients*.

8.9 You do not make unsolicited approaches to members of the public, with the exception of current or former *clients*, in order to advertise legal services provided by you, or your business or employer.

8.10 You ensure that *clients* understand whether and how the services you provide are regulated. This includes:

(a) explaining which activities will be carried out by you, as an *authorised person*;

(b) explaining which services provided by you, your business and your employer, and any *separate business* are regulated by an *approved regulator*; and

(c) ensuring that you do not represent any business or employer which is not authorised by the SRA, including any *separate business*, as being regulated by the SRA.

8.11 You ensure that *clients* understand the regulatory protections available to them.

Paragraphs 8.1 to 8.5 dealing with client identification and complaints handling are relatively straightforward. Where the Money Laundering, Terrorist Financing and Transfer of Funds (Information on the Payer) Regulations 2017, SI 2017/692 (MLR 2017) apply 'customer due diligence' is required and this issue is dealt with more fully in **Chapter 9**, which deals with relevant legislation affecting in-house practice. However, in all situations evidence of identity for clients is mandatory, and this will usually be provided through some form of photographic ID and household bills.

It should be noted that those who access legal services through a solicitor in an unregulated environment have the same right to complain and to refer a complaint to the Legal Ombudsman as those who instruct solicitors in private practice. Although the Legal Ombudsman's services are primarily aimed at individuals, others such as small businesses with a turnover of less than £2 million and clubs, charities and associations with an income of less than £1 million can access them. When taking up employment to provide legal services to the public, solicitors should consider mentioning this fact to the employer and should ensure that any proposed complaints handling process notifies clients of their right to make a complaint to the Legal Ombudsman.

The paragraphs which deal with client information and publicity are of particular note for in-house lawyers working for unauthorised bodies. They require that clients understand the regulatory protections that are available to them and whether and how the services are regulated. This means that as an in-house lawyer working in this environment you will need to ensure that your employer's website does not suggest the organisation is SRA regulated and, on an individual level, you will need to explain to clients which services will be provided by you as an authorised person. This would include any legal work done under your direct supervision by non-lawyers.

This section of the Code must also be read in conjunction with the SRA Transparency Rules 2018, which at rule 4.3 says:

> A *solicitor*, an *REL* or *RFL* who is providing legal services to the public or a section of the public other than through a firm that is regulated by the SRA:
>
> (a) where they are not required to meet the *MTC*, must before engagement inform all *clients* of this fact and specify that alternative insurance arrangements are in place if this is the case (together with information about the cover this provides, if requested); and
>
> (b) where applicable, must inform all *clients* that they will not be eligible to apply for a grant from the SRA Compensation Fund.

Rule 4.4 of these rules expressly disapplies rule 4.3 to those employed by not-for-profit organisations such as law centres. If, therefore, you are employed by an unauthorised body to provide legal services to the public you must make it clear to your clients that they will not have the benefit of indemnity insurance under the terms of the Solicitors Indemnity Rules, explain what other indemnity insurance arrangements your employer has in place and, if money is held by your employer for your clients, inform them that the SRA Compensation Fund will not be available to them.

5.6 INSTRUCTING LAWYERS IN PRIVATE PRACTICE

For those in-house lawyers who instruct firms to advise on and carry out aspects of legal work on behalf of their employers, it is useful to be familiar with the Codes (both the Code for Individuals and the Code for Firms) to know the requirements which private practice firms must meet. In-house teams that do this on a regular basis will usually have favoured firms that they know meet their requirements on expertise, costs and availability.

There are, however, certain high-risk areas of the Code where clear obligations are placed on firms in terms of their dealings with their clients, and where the in-house lawyer may need to be particularly alert. The in-house lawyer has an advantage over other clients in that the lawyer is likely to be more aware of those risk areas which can sour a relationship with a firm when things go wrong. These tend to revolve around failure to define a retainer clearly and failure to get clarity over costs. Other areas which may cause problems concern the use of information barriers and requests to agree to changes to the duty of disclosure.

Defining the work to be done is important at the outset of a matter and, in particular, defining what aspects of the work might be excluded. It may be the case that, for example, the firm instructed will not provide tax advice. This is something that in-house lawyers will need to check carefully to ensure that all aspects of their expectations match those of the firm instructed. Similarly, with regard to costs, setting out the billing procedures and ceilings for different stages of the work helps prevent costs running out of control.

As the matter progresses, instructions may become subject to 'mission creep' as unforeseen events arise which change the course of the matter. Where this occurs, the firm instructed should update the client on the changes and how these might affect costs. This, however, tends to be where problems can arise and the in-house lawyer needs to be alert to this and to be in touch with the firm about the changed nature of the instructions and the effect on costs.

When setting the terms of engagement, in-house lawyers also need to be alert to requests from a firm, which may wish to act for other clients in the same field and limit its duty of disclosure. Arrangements of this nature and those relating to the use of information barriers, whether formal or less formal, need to be discussed openly with the firm to ensure that the exact nature of the arrangements being proposed is fully understood. In-house lawyers may want assurances that their employer client will not find itself opposed by the firm in another matter.

Where formal information barriers are to be used, for example in relation to a bidding contest where the firm instructed also acts for other bidders or their financial backers, the firm instructed will need to comply with the stringent requirements in paragraphs 6.1 to 6.5 to allow it to act despite the conflict. In-house lawyers giving instructions in these circumstances will need to ensure that these requirements are met. Relevant issues must be explained by the firm and the employer client must give signed agreement to the arrangements.

5.7 ENFORCEMENT OF THE CODE

It is worth reflecting on the fact that instances of in-house lawyers being disciplined for breaches of the Code, or other regulatory requirements, have been extremely limited. This is undoubtedly for three main reasons.

First, the focus of the SRA's regulatory attention is largely on the firms it regulates and those that work within them. This is because the bulk of the SRA's resources are centred on assessing the risk that firms present to their clients and taking appropriate action to reduce that risk. This is even more the case since LSA 2007, which sets out regulatory objectives that govern all the activities of legal services regulators. These objectives are very much concerned with protecting the public as consumers of legal services. Historically speaking, in-house lawyers have not to any great extent provided services to the public, other than those employed in the not-for-profit sector.

Second, in relation to in-house practice, the lawyer is governed by a contract of employment, and the employer, to a large extent, polices the standards it requires. In practical terms, this tends to mean that the employer deals with inappropriate behaviour or incompetence through its own disciplinary processes.

Third, until now in-house lawyers have very rarely handled client money so the opportunity for default has been very limited.

With the relaxations which permit in-house lawyers to provide services to the public through unauthorised bodies, this new breed of in-house practice will, undoubtedly, come under the SRA's microscope. The SRA is all too aware of criticisms about possible risks to the public of allowing this type of practice and will no doubt be keeping a close eye on how it develops and any problems which may arise.

For the more conventional type of in-house practice where lawyers only do work for their employer and those closely related to their employer, the case of Alistair Brett, solicitor and the legal manager for The Times Newspapers Limited should act as a warning that those employed in-house are not immune to disciplinary action. The facts, in summary, are set out below.

Alistair Brett was the senior in-house solicitor for The Times Newspapers Limited and had acted for the paper in injunction proceedings over the alleged hacking of a policeman's email account. The background was that Brett was approached by a young journalist for the paper who claimed he had discovered the identity of a policeman who wrote a high-profile blog, under a pseudonym, about life in the police force. The blog was damaging to the police force and the journalist thought it was in the public interest to unmask the blogger. The reporter confessed the identity had been obtained by hacking. Brett advised the reporter that hacking was illegal and the story could not be published unless the identity of the blogger could be found through legal means. He also said that the blogger would have to be given notice and asked to comment if information which could be used to unmask him could be obtained legally.

The journalist subsequently sought to obtain the blogger's identity by identifying and cross-referring publicly available information. The blogger was contacted and told that the newspaper planned to run a story identifying him. He did not confirm or deny his identity as the blogger but instructed a firm of solicitors who sought an injunction preventing publication. The newspaper agreed not to run the story without giving 12 hours' notice. The notice of publication was served and the blogger asked the court for an injunction.

Prior to the hearing taking place, evidence was provided by the journalist in the form of a statement as to how he had gone about the process of identifying the blogger. The statement was drawn up by Brett. The solicitors acting for the blogger asked a direct question as to whether the journalist had obtained information by hacking the blogger's emails but this was not directly answered by Brett. The impression given by the statement was that the blogger's identity had only been obtained through information in the public domain. Neither leading nor junior counsel instructed by Brett were told about the hacking. They, therefore, proceeded on the basis that no hacking had been involved. Brett said nothing to correct this incorrect assumption. Leading counsel, in summing up said:

> The claimant's case ... was that this was old-fashioned breach of confidence and (the paper) must have learnt of his identity from a disclosure to it in breach of confidence. We now know that that is not right.

Brett's defence was that, in his view, the hacking became irrelevant once it could be established that the blogger's identity was ascertainable from publicly available material. He conceded he knew that the journalist's behaviour was probably likely to attract criminal sanctions.

The SRA brought proceedings against Brett in the SDT and the case was heard on 5 December 2013. The allegations were that he (a) failed to act with integrity, and (b) allowed the court to be misled. The SDT found the allegations to have been proved and suspended Brett from practice for a period of six months. He was also ordered to pay £30,000 costs.

CHAPTER 6

The SRA Accounts Rules

6.1 INTRODUCTION

'Client money' is defined in the SRA Accounts Rules and includes:

- money that clients pay you on account of your charges or third-party costs;
- any damages that your client receives as part of a settlement of a case;
- the assets of an estate that is being administered by your business;
- any other money that you are holding on your client's behalf to complete a transaction or for investment purposes.

At first glance it may seem that the Accounts Rules are one set of regulations that do not have any relevance to the in-house lawyer. This is not the case; because these apply very strict restrictions about the holding of client money, it is essential that in-house lawyers understand the prohibitions that apply to them.

The starting point is the Code for Individuals which applies to all solicitors, regardless of their type of practice, and states at paragraph 4.3:

> You do not personally hold *client money* save as permitted under regulation 10.2(b)(vii) of the Authorisation of Individuals Regulations, unless you work in an *authorised body*, or in an organisation of a kind *prescribed* under this rule on any terms that may be *prescribed* accordingly.

(Regulation 10.2 of the Authorisation of Individuals Regulations refers to the practice of freelance solicitors and is not relevant to the in-house lawyer.)

The significance of paragraph 4.3 is that solicitors working in unauthorised businesses (i.e. in businesses which are not SRA-authorised law firms) are prohibited from holding client money unless the organisation is positively designated as one in which solicitors are able to hold client money. Whether or not any designation applies to the in-house solicitor's employer is a fact that the solicitor should verify.

The most common examples of in-house lawyers holding client money are solicitors who are employed by law centres, charities and non-commercial advice services and give advice to and otherwise act for members of the public, and in such circumstances hold and receive client money. These organisations must secure the necessary permissions from the SRA.

The SRA has provided guidance on the position of solicitors working in the not-for-profit sector ('SRA Standards and Regulations guidance for the not for profit sector' – July 2019, **www.sra.org.uk/globalassets/documents/solicitors/not-for-profit-guidance.pdf?version=4a1ab8**). This is relevant to solicitors, registered European lawyers and registered foreign lawyers working in not-for-profit organisations such as law centres and other charities. The guidance includes the following statement:

> The SRA will prescribe 'non-commercial bodies' under the Legal Services Act 2007 (not for profit bodies, community interest companies and independent trade unions) as relevant organisations. This means that solicitors working in these organisations will be permitted to hold client money in their own name. If they choose to do so then all client money must be held in a client account and will be subject to the terms prescribed by the SRA.

In circumstances where the employing organisation is not prescribed, the employer should not ask an in-house solicitor to operate a bank account in the solicitor's own name, as this would place the individual in breach of the SRA's regulatory requirements. The solicitor is not prevented from being a signatory to a bank account held by the business in its own name but the client must understand that it is the business which is holding the money, not the solicitor, and that the business is not regulated and therefore regulatory protections will not be available. In order to comply with paragraph 8.11 of the Code for Individuals, the solicitor must provide information to clients to ensure they understand they do not have the regulatory protections that would be available if their money were held in a client account as defined by the SRA Accounts Rules.

6.2 WHICH IN-HOUSE LAWYERS ARE SUBJECT TO THE SRA ACCOUNTS RULES?

The Rules will therefore apply to solicitors in two specific circumstances:

1. If the SRA has prescribed that the employing organisation can operate a client account, in which event the prescription will provide a detailed commentary on the specific conditions which apply.
2. If the employing organisation has become an alternative business structure and therefore an authorised business. The Rules will apply in respect of activities regulated by the SRA in accordance with the terms of its licence.

'Client money' is defined in rule 2.1 as money held or received:

> (a) relating to *regulated services* delivered by you to a *client*;
> (b) on behalf of a third party in relation to *regulated services* delivered by you (such as money held as agent, stakeholder or held to the sender's order);
> (c) as a trustee or as the holder of a specified office or appointment, such as donee of a power of attorney, Court of Protection deputy or trustee of an occupational pension scheme;

(d) in respect of your *fees* and any unpaid *disbursements* if held or received prior to delivery of a bill for the same.

Fees are defined as meaning the solicitor's own charges or profit costs (including any VAT element). Disbursements are defined as meaning any costs or expenses paid or to be paid to a third party on behalf of the client or trust (including any VAT element) save for office expenses such as postage and courier fees.

Where the only client money you hold or receive falls within rule 2.1(d), and any money held for disbursements relates to costs or expenses incurred by you on behalf of your client and for which you are liable, and you do not for any other reason maintain a client account, then rule 2.2 states that this money does not need to be held in a client account provided that you have informed your client in advance of where and how the money will be held.

6.3 COMPLIANCE REQUIREMENTS AND THE HOLDING OF CLIENT MONEY

6.3.1 Operating a client account

Except in circumstances where rule 2.2 applies, an in-house lawyer who holds or receives client money must keep a client account and pay client money into that account promptly. The only exceptions are contained in rule 2.3:

(a) in relation to money falling within 2.1(c), to do so would conflict with your obligations under rules or regulations relating to your specified office or appointment;
(b) the *client money* represents payments received from the Legal Aid Agency for your *costs*; or
(c) you agree in the individual circumstances an alternative arrangement in writing with the *client*, or the third party, for whom the money is held.

Under rule 2.3(b) of the Accounts Rules 2019, payments received from the Legal Aid Agency do not need to be paid into a client account and can be paid into the employer's own account. This is a change from previous requirements, which required advance payments for disbursements to be put back into the client account if the party providing the professional services was not paid within a specified time. This requirement has now been removed.

However, the SRA gives this warning in the guidance for the not-for-profit sector:

> you should not hold payments from the LAA in your organisation's office account indefinitely as this may breach other requirements within the Code for Individuals and Principles. For example, if your organisation does not pay a fee promptly in order to retain the money in its business account and avoid increasing its overdraft and thereby delays the client's matter, this is likely to be a breach of Principle 7. The need to comply with the broad requirements within the Principles and Code for Individuals provides sufficient protection without the need for more detailed rules in relation to LAA payments.

If you have a contract with the LAA, you should check the relevant regulations and the LAA's contract requirements in relation to handling money.

Dealing with monies to be paid into client money, it is important to note that the term 'promptly' is not defined (whereas in previous versions of the SRA Accounts Rules, the requirement was to pay money into the client account on the day of receipt or the next working day). This allows flexibility to make business decisions as to what the term 'promptly' will mean.

The other rules which apply to the holding of client money are:

- Ordinarily, the money must be available on demand unless an alternative arrangement is agreed with the client (or a third party for whom the money is held) and this agreement is evidenced in writing.
- Client money must be returned promptly (again, this is not a defined term) to the client or the third party for whom the money is held as soon as there is no longer any proper reason to hold those funds.
- Client money must be kept separate from money belonging to the authorised body (except where you rely on rule 2.2) or the employer.
- You must allocate promptly any mixed payments to the correct client account or business account.
- Where you are holding client money and wish to use some or all of it to pay your costs, you must first give a bill of costs or other written notification of costs to the client or the paying party before a transfer is made.
- You must pay a fair sum of interest to the client or third party on any client money held, but you may come to a different arrangement if the client has given their informed consent.

The client account must be opened in accordance with rules 3.1 and 3.2 which dictate very specific requirements: it must be a bank account or a building society account at a branch (or a bank's or society's head office) in England and Wales and must be in the name of the authorised body. The name of the account must also include the word 'client' in full. It would be a reportable breach of the Rules if this word was not included or even if the word were abbreviated to, say, 'cl'.

There are two types of client account. First, there is the separate designated client account which is an account for money held in respect of a single client, other person or a trust and must include in its title (in addition to all other requirements) a reference to the client's identity. Second, any other type of client account is known as a general client account and is an account where monies belonging to more than one client are kept. Regardless of the type of client account, it is a requirement of the Rules that money must be immediately available unless the client gives contrary instructions or the circumstances clearly indicate otherwise.

The client account must not be used to provide banking facilities for the client or third parties. Payments into, and transfers or withdrawals from, a client account must be in respect of the delivery of regulated services.

This prohibition is significant. It was introduced as a mandatory rule in the SRA Accounts Rules 2011, which made it clear that solicitors should hold client money only where there is a specific need arising from the legal services being provided and that it is not the solicitor's role to provide banking facilities. Previously, this had been expressed as guidance and the fact that it was one of the few significant changes in the 2011 Rules cannot be underestimated. Its elevation to a mandatory rule reflected many decisions made by the Solicitors Disciplinary Tribunal (SDT) that supported the position that banking is not a proper legal service. Examples of the severity of such a misdemeanour can be shown in various cases which have come before the SDT, notably the case of *Wood and Burdett* (SDT 8669/2002). Using a solicitor's client account for services other than those arising from legal activities is likely also to increase the risk of being involved – either knowingly or unwittingly – in money laundering and other fraudulent activities.

Since 2011 there has been much case law and regulatory decision making which consolidates our understanding of this prohibition. For example, consider the case of *Fuglers & Others* v. *SRA* [2014] EWHC 179 (Admin) (QB). Fuglers LLP was instructed by Portsmouth Football Club at the time when the Club's bank account was suspended after a winding-up petition had been brought because of the Club's insolvency. The senior managers of Fuglers agreed to the use of the firm's client account by the Club. In excess of £10 million of the Club's money passed through the client account in a period of four months. The firm had favoured some unsecured creditors over others. This conduct was referred to the SDT. The firm was fined £50,000 and the two managers were fined a total of £25,000 because of the seriousness of the misconduct. The managers appealed this decision, asserting that the fines were excessive. The appeal was rejected and the court's decision included three reasons why client account use was subject to this prohibition:

1. The use of a client account as a banking facility is objectionable in itself; solicitors are not qualified to act as bankers nor regulated as bankers.
2. It increases the risk of money laundering taking place.
3. It increases the risk of insolvency.

Reflecting the regulatory concern about this, a warning notice was issued in 2014. This was updated in August 2018 and is available on the SRA website (**www.sra.org.uk/solicitors/guidance/warning-notices/Improper-use-of-client-account-as-a-banking-facility--Warning-notice**).

Warning notices contain regulatory risk content. The SRA requires lawyers to be aware of these: 'While this guidance does not form part of the SRA Standards and Regulations, we may have regard to it when exercising our regulatory functions.'

The warning notice is supported by various case studies to illustrate what is, and is not, likely to constitute a banking facility. For example, the following are examples of what are considered to be banking activities:

- holding unconnected money in a client account;

- execution-only escrow arrangements;
- lack of availability of UK banking facilities.

The following are more likely to be considered acceptable uses of the client account:

- holding rental deposits when acting for the landlord;
- development work and holding money;
- trust administration work.

Of equal importance is compliance with the requirements relating to withdrawals from client accounts, set out in rule 5.1.

Rule 5.1 sets out very specific and controlled circumstances in which client money may be withdrawn from a client account:

> (a) for the purpose for which it is being held;
> (b) following receipt of instructions from the *client*, or the third party for whom the money is held; or
> (c) on the *SRA's* prior written authorisation or in *prescribed* circumstances.

6.3.2 Accounting systems and records

The holding of client money and the operation of a client account trigger the need to have accounting systems and records, for the purposes of compliance with rule 8.1 of the Accounts Rules.

Rule 8.1 requires the following:

> You keep and maintain accurate, contemporaneous, and chronological records to:
>
> (a) record in client ledgers identified by the *client's* name and an appropriate description of the matter to which they relate:
>
> (i) all receipts and payments which *client money* on the client side of the client ledger account;
> (ii) all receipts and payments which are not *client money* and bills of *costs* including transactions through the *authorised body's* accounts on the business side of the client ledger account;
>
> (b) maintain a list of all the balances shown by the client ledger accounts of the liabilities to *clients* (and third parties), with a running total of the balances; and
> (c) provide a cash book showing a running total of all transactions through *client accounts* held or operated by you.

Holding client money triggers the need to obtain bank or building society statements, as the case may be, both in respect of the client account and the business account. Rule 8.2 stipulates that a solicitor must, at least every five weeks, either obtain hard copy statements (or duplicate statements permitted in lieu of the originals) from banks, building societies or other financial institutions, or obtain and save in the accounting records, in a format that cannot be altered, an electronic version of the bank's, building society's or other financial institution's online record. Each statement or electronic version must begin at the end of the previous statement. Failure to keep such records is a reportable breach of the Accounts Rules.

Reconciliations must take place at least once every five weeks to compare the balance on the client cash account(s) with the balances shown on the statements and passbooks (after allowing for all unpresented items) of all general client accounts and separate designated client accounts. In authorised firms the reconciliation must be signed off by the Compliance Officer for Finance and Administration (COFA) or a manager. No doubt, any unauthorised organisation which is granted SRA permission to operate a client account will be given specific guidance as to the regulatory expectations which will apply to it.

In addition, solicitors must keep readily accessible a central record or file of copies of all bills given or sent by them (other than those relating entirely to activities not regulated by the SRA); and all other written notifications of costs given or sent by them (other than those relating entirely to activities not regulated by the SRA).

All accounting records must be kept for at least six years (rule 13.1). The SRA has published guidance 'Helping you keep accurate client accounting records' (**www.sra.org.uk/solicitors/guidance/ethics-guidance/helping-you-keep-accurate-client-accounting-records**).

6.3.3 Accountant's report

Perhaps the most onerous aspect of the Accounts Rules for an in-house lawyer who holds client money is the need to comply with the SRA's requirements for the filing of an accountant's report as set out in rule 12.

However, these provisions have been modified as discussed below.

Rule 12.2 states that an accountant's report is not required in the following circumstances:

> (a) all of the *client money* held or received during an *accounting period* is money received from the Legal Aid Agency; or
>
> (b) in the *accounting period*, the statement or passbook balance of *client money* you have held or received does not exceed:
>
> (i) an average of £10,000; and
>
> (ii) a maximum of £250,000,
>
> or the equivalent in foreign currency.

Rule 12.4 gives the SRA a discretion to apply the requirement where the 'SRA considers that it is otherwise in the public interest to do so', and the SRA Guidance for the not-for-profit sector states as follows:

> The provisions in the Accounts Rules relating to Accountant's Reports will not generally apply to the not for profit sector as we do not think that it is necessary to receive reports from solicitors in this sector as standard. However, we can request a report in exceptional circumstances under rule 12.4: ...

Anyone believing that they are able to rely on rule 12.4 and this guidance note should seek clarification from the SRA.

In any other circumstance, qualified reports must be filed with the SRA.

The SRA has published two guidance notes which will assist with this aspect of the holding of client money:

- Accountant's report and the exemption to obtain one (August 2017 and updated July 2019) – **www.sra.org.uk/solicitors/guidance/ethics-guidance/accountant-s-report-and-the-exemption-to-obtain-one**.
- Planning for and completing an accountant's report (August 2017 and updated July 2019) – **www.sra.org.uk/solicitors/guidance/ethics-guidance/planning-for-and-completing-an-accountant-s-report**.

6.3.4 Dealings with other money belonging to clients or third parties

In some circumstances a solicitor may operate joint accounts or the client's own account. In these circumstances rules 9 and 10 apply a modified version of the accounting requirements which must be observed. The SRA has published a guidance note to assist with joint accounts and record-keeping, available from the SRA website (**www.sra.org.uk/solicitors/guidance/ethics-guidance/joint-accounts-and-record-keeping**).

6.3.5 Third-party managed account

The third-party managed account (TPMA) was introduced in the latest version of the SRA Accounts Rules at rules 11.1 and 11.2. According to the Glossary, this is:

> an account held at a bank or building society in the name of a third party which is an authorised payment institution, a small payment institution that has chosen to implement safeguarding arrangement in accordance with the Payment Services Regulations or an *EEA* authorised payment institution (as each defined in Regulation 2 of the Payment Services Regulations 2009) regulated by the *FCA*, in which monies are owned beneficially by the third party, and which is operated upon terms agreed between the third party, you and your client as an escrow payment service.

The Rules allow you to enter into an arrangement with a client to use a TPMA:

> for the purpose of receiving payments from or on behalf of, or making payments to or on behalf of, the *client* in respect of *regulated services* delivered by you to the *client*, only if:
>
> (a) use of the account does not result in you receiving or holding the *client's* money; and
>
> (b) you take reasonable steps to ensure, before accepting instructions, that the *client* is informed of and understands:
>
> (i) the terms of the contractual arrangements relating to the use of the *third party managed account*, and in particular how any *fees* for use of the *third party managed account* will be paid and who will bear them; and

(ii) the *client's* right to terminate the agreement and dispute payment requests made by you.

The SRA published guidance on TPMAs in December 2017, updated in July 2019, which is available from the SRA website (**www.sra.org.uk/solicitors/guidance/ethics-guidance/third-party-managed-accounts**).

CHAPTER 7

New regulatory freedoms for in-house practice

7.1 INTRODUCTION

The SRA Practice Framework Rules 2011 previously governed the ways in which lawyers regulated by the SRA could provide their services. These rules had particular application to in-house practice as they restricted those bodies and individuals to whom in-house lawyers could provide services as part of their employment. Rule 4 prevented in-house lawyers from providing, as part of their employment, legal services to anyone other than their employer and those closely associated with their employer. To give examples, those employed by a company could act for other companies within the group and those employed in local government could provide services to any individual or organisation to whom, or to which, their local authority was statutorily empowered to provide legal services. There were, however, other in-house situations where these restrictions were difficult to apply. For example, those acting for members of an association had to deal with restrictions on issues such as when services could be charged for, or even who could be classified as members. Things became even more complicated for those employed by commercial providers of telephone legal advice services because of issues about how much follow-up work could be done to support the telephone advice.

All those regulatory prohibitions have now been swept aside. The SRA Standards and Regulations 2019 repeal the Practice Framework Rules, including the rule 4 restrictions which had for so long governed for whom in-house lawyers could act. This is arguably the biggest change brought about by the new rules and is likely to be a game changer in terms of how the legal services market operates in the future. The reason for this is that a new and wide-ranging form of in-house practice has been created, which allows SRA-regulated lawyers to be employed by companies or other organisations or individuals which, or who, are not regulated by an approved legal services regulator. As part of that employment they are free to provide legal services to the public provided those services are not 'reserved legal activities'.

7.2 THE EFFECT OF LSA 2007 AND OTHER STATUTORY RESTRICTIONS ON IN-HOUSE PRACTICE

7.2.1 LSA 2007

With the repeal of the Practice Framework Rules, it must not be overlooked that there remain some important statutory restrictions on the provision of legal services which continue to govern in-house lawyers. Foremost is LSA 2007 which singles out 'reserved legal activities' as being core legal activities which must be provided through a fully regulated environment. Under LSA 2007, where services described as 'reserved legal activities' are provided by a non-lawyer entity to 'the public or a section of the public' ('the relevant activity') the entity must be licensed as an alternative business structure (ABS). Commercial bodies which provide 'the relevant activity' must, therefore, be licensed as ABSs or face criminal prosecution. There is an exception. Not-for-profit organisations, described as 'special bodies' in LSA 2007, have not been brought into the ABS regime because they are viewed as low risk by the Legal Services Board, which has decided at the moment to take no steps to require them to become ABSs. There is more on this in **Chapter 8**.

One of the problems in applying the law is that 'the public or a section of the public' is not defined in LSA 2007. This may create difficulties for some organisations and their solicitors that provide legal services which may include reserved legal activities. The main example concerns membership associations formed for the specific purpose of furthering their members' activities or interests. In other words, they are a defined group of people with a common purpose who usually pay a membership fee for certain privileges, such as legal advice. The pertinent issue is: when are 'members' classified as 'the public or a section of the public'? This is something which has not yet been tested by the courts. However, given the consequences of getting it wrong, any in-house lawyer employed by an 'association' or similar organisation would be well advised to obtain a legal opinion where they have any doubt about their situation.

The Lord Chancellor can be asked to make an order defining what does or does not constitute a section of the public but at present no steps have been taken to ask him to do so. LSA 2007 itself excludes a class of individuals who would generally be regarded as the public, or a section of the public, when it removes from regulation 'relevant activities' offered by independent trade unions to their members. This does raise the question of why association members and independent trade union members need less protection than others do and may be an issue which will require further thought in the future.

'Reserved legal activities' as defined in LSA 2007 are:

- advocacy;
- conduct of litigation;
- reserved instrument activities (conveyancing);
- probate activities;

- notarial activities; and
- administration of oaths.

It should be noted that the Legal Services Board (LSB) can recommend to the Lord Chancellor that the list of reserved activities be extended. An attempt to include will writing was rejected. It is possible that the list could be extended to include other legal activities, although this seems unlikely given that the LSB has recently approved the SRA's rule relaxations which allow in-house lawyers to provide all non-reserved legal activities to the public. However, if these relaxations provide evidence of unacceptable risk to the public this may be revisited.

LSA 2007, s.15 sets out the position with regard to when in-house lawyers and their employers can and cannot provide reserved legal activities. In a nutshell it:

- prevents both in-house lawyers and their employers from providing these activities to 'the public or a section of the public (with or without a view to profit)';
- allows in-house lawyers to provide these activities for their employer and others provided they do not constitute the public; and
- makes trade unions providing these activities to their members an exception.

Not-for-profit organisations, defined as 'special bodies', which provide reserved legal activities to the public are excepted from these provisions unless required to be licensed. As has previously been mentioned, the LSB seems in no hurry to require them to be licensed as ABSs.

If, as an in-house lawyer, you are doing pro bono work you need to exercise care if it is likely to involve conducting reserved legal activities. If the work is being done as part of your employment, LSA 2007 will be relevant. This is because your employer cannot provide these services to the public unless licensed as an ABS. Whether the work is done as part of your employment will be a matter of fact.

The SRA issued guidance to rule 4.10 of the SRA Practice Framework Rules 2011 concerning pro bono work for those employed in-house and compliance with LSA 2007. Although rule 4 has now been repealed by the SRA Standards and Regulations, the guidance associated with pro bono work and compliance with the LSA 2007 is still valid and is set out below:

> To determine whether you can undertake reserved legal activities ... one question will be whether the activities to be undertaken can be regarded as part of the business of the employer. Relevant factors are likely to be:
>
> (a) relevancy of such work to the employer's business;
> (b) whether the work is required of the employee by the employer;
> (c) how often such work is carried out;
> (d) where such work is carried out;
> (e) when such work is carried out;
> (f) whether such work is explicitly carried out on the employer's behalf;
> (g) who provides the necessary professional indemnity insurance;
> (h) the extent to which the employer relies on or publicises such work;

(i) whether the employer provides management, training or supervision in relation to such work;
(j) whether the employer specifically rewards the employee in any way in relation to such work;
(k) how many employees carry out the work, and the overall proportion of their time spent on such work;
(l) the extent to which such work complements or enhances the employer's business.

All the circumstances, and the context, will be critical to your decision about whether you may act, for example the work will not necessarily be part of the employer's business merely because it is carried out in office hours, or at the employer's premises.

There will be some situations which are likely to be easier to judge. If there is a clear relationship with the employer's business, acting will not be permissible. For example, you are likely to be prevented from acting:

(A) where the employer describes its business as including the provision of pro bono services;
(B) where the work may boost the employer's business by providing extra business opportunities or creating contacts.

Sections 14 and 16 of LSA 2007 make it an offence for employer and employee to provide reserved activities where not permitted to do so.

The legal position means that some employers and their legal departments may need to be licensed as an ABS to operate within the law. The eligibility requirements and the licensing process for those whose employers need to be licensed as an ABS will be considered in more detail in **Chapter 8**.

Other work which in-house lawyers may not be able to provide to the public is:

- immigration work – unless the business is separately authorised by the Office of the Immigration Services Commissioner;
- claims management services – unless the business is separately authorised for these services by the Financial Conduct Authority (FCA);
- certain financial services or activities – unless the business is separately authorised for these by the FCA.

7.2.2 Local government

For those employed in local government, there are certain statutory restrictions on which individuals or bodies they can provide services to.

Although those employed in local government are no longer subject to SRA regulatory restrictions regarding for whom they can act, they are subject to legal restrictions affecting their employer. One of the key powers is the Local Authorities (Goods and Services) Act 1970. This Act enables local authorities to:

- supply goods or materials;
- provide any administrative, professional or technical service;
- use vehicles, plant or apparatus and appropriate staff; and
- undertake works of maintenance;

for other local authorities and many other organisations designated as 'public bodies' by other statutes and statutory instruments. These include the Local Government Acts 1972 and 2000 and the Local Authorities (Arrangements for the Discharge of Functions) (England) Regulations 2012, SI 2012/1019. The list of 'public bodies' includes police bodies, fire services, educational establishments, housing associations, 'community associations', health bodies and others.

The Localism Act 2011 gave increased powers and greater flexibility to local authorities to decide how best to deal with housing and services in their area. The extent to which this extends the previous powers is not entirely clear. However, it is for local authorities and their lawyers to decide whom they can act for within the relevant statutory constraints.

7.3 PRACTICE THROUGH UNAUTHORISED BODIES

Practice through unauthorised bodies will open up increased and novel opportunities for in-house practice and it will be interesting to see how this new legal sector unfolds. It is a form of practice which, to all intents and purposes, mimics private practice in terms of the obligations the lawyer will owe to the clients. It does, however, undoubtedly carry new risks because the scope for tension between the unregulated employer and the regulated lawyer will be greatly increased. Commercial pressures from employers which are subject to few regulatory restrictions beyond the general law may well, on occasions, clash with the highly regulated regime to which the in-house lawyer is subject when providing services to the public. As a solicitor working in this environment you will need to be very clear about what your regulatory obligations are. You may also find that there could be an element of 'back door regulation' by the SRA, which puts pressure on you to control your employer.

The Code of Conduct for Individuals and the Transparency Rules set out certain information that you are required to give the client regarding the fact that although you are regulated, the company providing the legal services is not, which will lead to a loss of regulatory protections, and what these losses are. The SRA has also issued three sets of guidance which provide more information on what will be expected of you and your employer.

- For lawyers: **www.sra.org.uk/solicitors/guidance/ethics-guidance/unregulated-organisations---giving-information-to-clients**.
- Their employers: **www.sra.org.uk/solicitors/guidance/ethics-guidance/unregulated-organisations---for-employers-of-sra-regulated-lawyers**.
- On the subject of conflicts of interest: **www.sra.org.uk/solicitors/guidance/ethics-guidance/unregulated-organisations---conflict-and-confidentiality**.

The Law Society has also issued detailed guidance for this new in-house role: **www.lawsociety.org.uk/support-services/advice/practice-notes/solicitors-offering-legal-services-to-public-from-unregulated-entities**.

This will be looked at below in conjunction with the relevant rule changes.

7.3.1 Which rules apply to this form of practice

The SRA Principles, the Code for Individuals and the Transparency Rules are the key starting points. The Principles set out high levels of ethical conduct applying to all forms of practice and are dealt with in full in **Chapter 5**. The Code and the Transparency Rules set out specific information which must be given by lawyers to clients of unregulated firms.

Of particular relevance to in-house practice will be paragraphs 8.1 to 8.11 of the Code for Individuals. It applies to those 'providing services to the public or a section of the public' regardless of whether this is in a regulated or unregulated environment. Paragraph 8.6 sets out the general requirements about giving information to clients. This must be done in a way they understand and enable them to make informed decisions about the services they need, how their matter will be handled, and the options available to them.

Paragraphs 8.2 to 8.5 ('Complaints handling') and the SRA's guidance confirm that they apply to those working in-house. This means that in-house solicitors must give clients information about the complaints handling arrangements available to them. This must include giving them information about their right to make a complaint to the Legal Ombudsman and when this can be done.

Paragraphs 8.10 and 8.11 are particularly important to in-house practice as they flag up the need to be clear to clients about what regulatory protections apply. Paragraph 8.10 states that solicitors must ensure that clients understand whether and how the services they are to receive are regulated. In particular, this must include:

(a) explaining which activities will be carried out by you, as an *authorised person*;
(b) explaining which services provided by you, your business or employer and any *separate business* are regulated by an *approved regulator*; and
(c) ensuring that you do not represent any business or employer which is not authorised by the *SRA*, including any *separate business*, as being regulated by the *SRA*.

Ensuring that clients understand how the services they are to receive are regulated places a heavy burden on those employed in-house. They will need to explain clearly to their clients, some of whom may be vulnerable or have a poor understanding of English, that although the lawyer as an individual is SRA-regulated, the firm is not. The obvious way to make this clear is to provide information on the employer's website, particularly in any section dealing with the company's legal services, and in the terms of business issued to the client. However, if there is any doubt about the client's ability to read or understand this information, it might be necessary to explain it in person and record that this has been done.

Where two or more different services are being provided by the employer to the client, one of the most difficult aspects of the requirements of paragraph 8.10 might be making clear exactly which work falls into the 'legal services' category and is, therefore, regulated, and which work falls outside the regulated net. This may need some careful delineation in a client care letter.

Paragraph 8.11 goes one step further and states that you must 'ensure that clients understand the regulatory protections available to them'. Again, this will need to be explained quite clearly in the firm's terms of business or even in person. Clients must be told that, although the individual solicitor acting for them, or supervising their legal work, is regulated and obliged to meet certain regulatory obligations, the company is not, and that this results in some loss of protection. The exact losses which must be explained are that:

- client money cannot be held by the solicitor (this is prohibited by paragraph 4.3 of the Code for Individuals) and must, therefore, be held outside a solicitor's client account;
- there is no access to the SRA Compensation Fund (this is a requirement of rule 4.3(b) of the Transparency Rules); and
- indemnity insurance which meets the minimum terms and conditions required under the SRA Indemnity Rules is not available. If there is alternative indemnity insurance cover, this must be explained. (This requirement is to be found in rule 4.3(a) of the Transparency Rules.)

This will inevitably require some explanation of the purpose of the Compensation Fund and the minimum terms and conditions under the Indemnity Rules, in order to ensure clients understand what it is that they are to lose.

Other usual information must be given to clients, including costs information which must be 'the best possible information about how their matter will be priced and, both at the time of engagement and when appropriate as their matter progresses, about the overall cost of the matter and any *costs* incurred' (paragraph 8.7). See **Chapter 5** for more detail.

What the guidance adds to the rules

The guidance for lawyers and for their employers tries to expand on the standards and rules and smooth over some of the difficulties created by having two Codes of Conduct. The fact that the Code for Firms does not apply may potentially create problems for the in-house situation. For example, there is no obligation to have systems and procedures under the Code for Individuals. However, as this Code includes standards relating to client confidentiality, conflicts of interests, client care and undertakings it might be difficult for a lawyer as an employee of an unauthorised body to demonstrate compliance with these standards without having appropriate systems and procedures in place. This is likely to be especially so where the lawyer is responsible for supervising staff providing legal services. In the SRA's guidance for employers, the SRA makes it clear that it would expect to see appropriate systems and procedures when it says:

> Solicitors bring with them the advantages of professional training and accreditation in law, and of adherence to the ethical and professional standards set out in our regulatory arrangements. These arrangements will benefit and protect both you and your customers, but you will want to ensure that you have systems and policies in place within your business to enable the solicitor to comply with these. You may wish to discuss how best to do that with the solicitors that you employ, as well as considering this guidance and the other resources referred to in it.

Ideally, any prospective employee solicitor should direct their employer to the SRA's guidance when negotiating their contract of employment. It would be sensible to ensure that the contract makes it clear that the employer will do nothing to prevent the solicitor employee from meeting their professional obligations. Key messages in the employer's guidance are that the business can in no way indicate that it is SRA-authorised or regulated, that the solicitor cannot hold client money in the solicitor's own name, that there must be a complaints handling system and that clients must be told of their right to take complaints to the Legal Ombudsman and must also be informed that the business does not have indemnity insurance under the terms of the SRA rules. The guidance also flags up the importance of the SRA Principles, in particular those of independence and integrity. It lists key obligations arising from the Code for Individuals, such as the duty of confidentiality and the duty not to act where there is a conflict of interests. It also lists those activities that the in-house solicitor cannot provide which, in addition to the reserved legal activities, includes immigration work, claims management work and financial services, unless the business is appropriately regulated for these activities. Finally, it reminds the employer that the solicitor must have a practising certificate and keep their competence and professional knowledge up to date.

The guidance for solicitors is clearly intended to bring clarity to some other difficult situations which might arise, such as where a solicitor acts for a client as part of a joint team which includes lawyers regulated by other approved regulators. The difficulty in that situation is to try to explain what aspects of the service that the client is to receive will be conducted by or under the supervision of the solicitor and, therefore, SRA-regulated. The guidance makes the point that this will be easier to determine if the solicitor is supervising a discrete or particular aspect of the case. It goes on to say that 'if it is not possible to draw a clear boundary around the services provided by you or other authorised lawyers, then the client should be informed that you will be carrying on this work jointly with others and you will be accountable to us for the work as a whole'. What the guidance does not touch upon is the even more difficult situation where legal work and non-legal work might be carried out for the client by a multi-disciplinary team. In that situation the solicitor would have to ensure that the work they are to carry out, or which is to be carried out under their supervision, is very clearly defined in the client care letter.

The SRA's guidance highlights other obligations that it considers important to in-house solicitors. This is:

- 'Telling clients about any referral fees that you or the firm have paid for the case, or about any financial interest any introducer has in referring the matter to you.'
- 'Making clients aware of all information material to their matter of which you have knowledge, subject to some limited exceptions.'
- 'Making sure that clients receive the best possible information about how their matter will be priced and, both at the time of engagement and when appropriate as their matter progresses, about the likely overall cost of the matter and any costs incurred.'
- 'If you or your employer is connected to an SRA-regulated firm (for example, one firm owns the other) such that your employer is a separate business, then paragraph 5.3 states that the client must give informed consent for any matter to be divided between the regulated firm and the separate business.'

Finally, the SRA has issued detailed guidance on the subject of conflicts of interest and the duty of confidentiality and situations which may affect in-house practice. It starts by making the point that, as a solicitor, you cannot act if your own interests conflict with those of the client and gives examples of conflicts, two of which are specifically referable to the in-house situation:

- 'Your role as an employee – for example a client asks for advice in relation to a dispute involving your employer or a fellow employee.'
- 'Your own conduct or that of your employer – for example the wrong advice has been given to the client or the wrong action taken on their behalf.'

It also gives examples of client conflict situations which include these:

- 'Where the matter itself concerns a dispute between the clients. For example, you cannot advise both sides in a dispute between a landlord and tenant, or a debt recovery matter.'
- 'Two clients seeking separately to purchase a particular asset or to be awarded a particular contract.'
- 'Acting for an investor and the scheme in which they will be investing.'
- 'One client selling or leasing an asset to another client.'
- 'Agreeing a commercial contract between two clients.'

More information on the application of the conflict standards appears in **Chapter 5**. Assessing conflicts in-house is exactly the same as in private practice. The only difference may lie in convincing the employer to accept the importance of refusing instructions where a conflict is identified.

7.3.2 What are the risks new prospective in-house lawyers of unauthorised bodies should be considering?

It is worth emphasising that this is very new territory and is not something to be embraced without careful thought about (a) the nature of the prospective employment and employer and (b) the detail of what the role will entail. First and foremost, in-house solicitors must comply with all their regulatory obligations, which may create tension with some employers, so points to consider when deciding whether to take a post may include these:

- Doing background checks on the employer – who owns the company, do they have any issues of a financial/criminal nature and what sort of reputation does the company have? Although the SRA does not have any power over the company, it may well take the view that a lawyer providing services for a company which has acted disreputably (e.g. discriminating unlawfully, overcharging, failing to account for money held) was acting in breach of principle 2 (maintaining trust in you and the provision of legal services).
- Including a term in the contract of employment making clear that the lawyer's professional obligations are paramount and should not be overridden by the company.
- Obtaining clarity in the contract of employment about what legal services are to be provided (are you competent to handle them?)
- What pressure are you likely to be subjected to when being asked to refer clients to other services offered by your employer? Will you be free to refuse where you do not think it is in the client's best interests?
- Ensuring that, if you are to have a supervisory role, it is clear who you will be supervising and the work they will be carrying out – again it would be helpful to have this set out in your contract. This is potentially a contentious area, concerning just how far in-house lawyers are to be considered responsible for supervising the legal work of paralegals working alongside them under paragraph 3.5 of the new Code for Individuals. If the position is unclear, the SRA may take the view that if paralegals look to a lawyer for advice and support, the lawyer is therefore supervising them even if the lawyer's job title does not include words suggesting a supervisory or managerial role.
- The assumption has to be that all those working under the lawyer's supervision must similarly comply with the Code and, for example, not act where there is a conflict of interests and must keep client affairs confidential. Although there is no requirement in the Code for Individuals (unlike the Code for Firms) for lawyers to have systems and procedures in place to deal with compliance it seems clear that the SRA would expect this as a measure of demonstrating how compliance is achieved. This is something which should be raised and cleared with your prospective employer.
- Consider whether the client will need to rely on legal professional privilege. If this is a possibility, you need to consider (a) whether privilege applies and (b) if not, whether the client should be referred elsewhere to get the benefit of

privileged advice. If privilege is likely to be important, it would be very difficult to meet principle 7 (acting in the client's best interests) by acting where privilege did not apply to the advice to be given. It should be noted that the SRA has declined to offer an opinion on the circumstances in which privilege would apply, on the basis that this legal advice is outside its remit. If there is doubt over this, consider suggesting to your employer that counsel's opinion should be obtained to clarify the issue.

- Consider the indemnity insurance arrangements that the employer is offering. It would be very unwise to accept employment where some form of equivalent insurance is not provided. You must be allowed to explain to clients that the terms under which indemnity insurance is offered by authorised law firms is not available.
- Complaints handling procedures – what does your employer have in mind? The Code for Individuals requires you to have a complaints handling procedure, and your clients must be told about the Legal Ombudsman and their rights in that regard.
- Is client money to be held by the employer? If so, what arrangements are in place to ensure it is kept separate and that there is proper record-keeping? As an in-house lawyer, you will not be able to hold client money in your own name but your obligations to your clients are likely to require that you are satisfied that there is no risk to their money.

This is not an exhaustive list but should give some idea of the issues that may arise when considering in-house practice as a lawyer offering legal services to the public.

This is a new area of practice where, as yet, not all the possible difficulties for lawyers and their clients may be clear. What must be anticipated is that the SRA will be keeping a very close eye on how it develops. It may be that some form of thematic review will be undertaken to assess compliance.

CHAPTER 8

How to become an ABS

8.1 INTRODUCTION

The SRA is designated a licensing body and it has been accepting applications from entities wanting to be licensed since early 2012. It is worth recapping that all non-lawyer owned and/or managed organisations wishing to provide reserved legal services to the public must be licensed to do so and must employ lawyers who are authorised to provide those services. There is an exception. The not-for-profit sector of law centres and advice centres, community interest companies and independent trade unions are treated differently. Called 'special bodies' by LSA 2007, they are subject to transitional arrangements which allow them to provide reserved legal services until the Lord Chancellor orders the end of these arrangements. The Legal Services Board (LSB) has deferred asking the Lord Chancellor to make an order because it considers these organisations are sufficiently low risk that they do not need to be brought within the licensing regime at present. The SRA has issued guidance with a flowchart to help in-house lawyers decide whether their employer needs to be authorised – see **www.sra.org.uk/solicitors/guidance/ethics-guidance/does-my-employer-need-to-be-authorised-by-an-approved-regulator-**.

Since the licensing regime came into effect, some commercial organisations have elected to become alternative business structures (ABSs) or to set up a separate related body as an ABS to conduct reserved legal activities for their clients. For example, licences have been granted to mutual insurance companies that wish to conduct claims through the courts for their members rather than refer them to firms of solicitors. Some local authorities have also set up ABSs to do their legal work, and in order to be able to offer legal services to other local authorities and related public sector bodies.

This chapter will outline which professional bodies can license ABSs and give an overview of the SRA's application process as it often falls to the in-house solicitor to make the application on behalf of the employer.

8.2 WHO CAN LICENSE ALTERNATIVE BUSINESS STRUCTURES?

Organisations need to become ABSs if they decide to offer reserved legal activities to the public or if they are already offering non-reserved legal services to the public and want to add reserved activities. Any lawyer employed by an entity that decides to sell its legal services to others needs to be very aware of the obligations set out in LSA 2007 and the penalties for providing services in breach of its requirements. This is dealt with in more detail in **Chapter 7**.

Where a licence is necessary the organisation will need to decide which licensing body is most appropriate for its needs. Currently, the Law Society (through the SRA), the Bar Council (through the Bar Standards Board), the Council for Licensed Conveyancers (CLC), the Institute of Chartered Accountants in England and Wales (ICAEW) and Intellectual Property Regulation Board (IPReg) are licensing bodies. However, an important consideration is that not all licensing bodies can license the full range of reserved legal activities. The SRA and the BSB are able to do so (with the exception of notarial services) but the CLC can only license reserved instrument activities, probate activities and the administration of oaths, the ICAEW can license probate activities and IPReg can license rights of audience, conduct of litigation and the administration of oaths. The Chartered Institute of Legal Executives (CILEx) is currently applying for licensing body status. Given that the LSB has to approve the rules of each licensing body, they all have similar application processes but the costs of the application and the subsequent costs of being regulated can differ, so this is a factor to be considered by any organisation looking to become an ABS. The regulatory regime also varies between regulators and this is also worth taking into account. It should also be noted that an organisation employing a solicitor does not have to be licensed by the SRA, although the individual solicitor will continue to be subject to SRA regulation. The rest of this chapter will, however, focus on the SRA's procedures for licensing ABSs as the vast majority of applications are made to the SRA rather than to the other regulators.

8.3 ELIGIBILITY

Rule 1.1 of the SRA Authorisation of Firms Rules 2019 requires ABS applicants to be a 'licensable body' and to have at least one manager who is an authorised person. LSA 2007, s.72 states that a body is licensable if a non-authorised person or another body is a manager or has an interest in it. The term 'manager' is defined as meaning a partner of a partnership, a member of a limited liability partnership (LLP) or a director of a company. A non-authorised person means someone who is not authorised to carry out a reserved legal activity.

Rule 1.3 requires that companies applying to be authorised must be incorporated in England and Wales, Scotland or Northern Ireland under Parts 1 and 2 of the Companies Act 2006; or in an Establishment Directive state and registered as an overseas company under Part 34 of the Companies Act 2006; or be incorporated and registered in an Establishment Directive state as a societas Europaea. A practising address in England and Wales is also essential.

Legal teams and their employers should have little difficulty in meeting these basic criteria.

8.4 COST OF APPLYING

The SRA's application fee is, at present, calculated as follows:

1. An initial payment of £2,000 (this is based on a daily rate of £600).
2. A payment of £150 in relation to each candidate who needs to be approved as a manager, owner and/or compliance officer (an authorised role holder).
3. If the SRA's costs in considering the application exceed the amounts specified above, any additional costs will be charged at a daily rate of £600.
4. If it is necessary for the SRA to seek external assistance, the full cost of that assistance will be charged to the applicant body.

Those licensed by the SRA are also required to pay an initial periodical fee on authorisation, which is calculated by reference to the firm's estimated turnover (using a formula set by the SRA), paying one-twelfth of that amount in relation to each month or part of a month between the date of authorisation and 31 October on the year in question. It should be noted that the SRA's costs as a regulator are now substantially recovered through a periodical fee paid annually by each authorised firm rather than from the practising certificate fee of individuals.

By way of comparison, the CLC's initial application fee is £1,200 plus £80 per hour for additional work where the application is complex. However, as noted above, the CLC can only license a firm that limits its reserved activities to conveyancing and probate.

8.5 HOW TO APPLY TO THE SRA

Since first licensing ABSs in 2012, the SRA has made its forms and the application process shorter and significantly less bureaucratic.

The application process is governed by the SRA Application, Notice, Review and Appeal Rules 2019 and the SRA Authorisation of Firms Rules 2019. The Application, Notice, Review and Appeal Rules introduced the same processes for all types of applications made to the SRA, whether by individuals or firms, under its rules and regulations. The Authorisation of Firms Rules adds extra requirements for authorisation applications and sets out the eligibility requirements for applicants.

Rule 1.1 of the Application, Notice, Review and Appeal Rules sets out what an application must comprise, namely:

- the prescribed form, correctly completed;

- any prescribed fee or charge for the application; and
- any information and documents which the SRA may prescribe or reasonably require.

Rule 1.2 states that an application will only be considered to be made when the SRA has received all payments, information and documents relating to it. If any of the information changes the applicant must immediately notify the SRA.

The Authorisation of Firms Rules require the SRA to give notice of its decision within six months of the application being made, although an extension notice can be served extending the six months to nine months. In reality, with any relatively well put together application a decision can be anticipated in under three months.

The rules also require that, in essence, an applicant's managers, interest holders and governance arrangements are suitable to run a legal services business and that the applicant will meet the regulatory objectives of the LSA 2007.

The 'prescribed form' required by rule 1 is, in fact, several different forms which need to be completed by the applicant body, its non-lawyer owners and managers and the Compliance Officer for Legal Practice (COLP) and the Compliance Officer for Finance and Administration (COFA). There are also forms to be completed through which the SRA collects information about compliance with the Money Laundering Regulations 2017 and the financial services activities of the applicant. All the forms can be downloaded from the SRA's website, **www.sra.org.uk/solicitors/firm-based-authorisation/authorisation-recognition.page**.

The SRA also provides basic guidance on completing the forms, as follows:

- FA1 – this is the form for the applicant firm and asks for all the background information about the applicant entity and those who own and will manage it. It is broken down as follows:

  1. Applicant details and contact person (including practising addresses and turnover).
  2. Post and role holder details (details of managers, owners and compliance officers and whether deemed approved).
  3. Organisation information (structure chart, company documents, details of any separate businesses and turnover).
  4. Areas of work (categories of work, if the applicant is to be a multi-disciplinary practice, if it will undertake financial services, claims management services or services subject to money laundering regulations).
  5. Insurance (the proposed arrangements must be set out with an offer of insurance annexed).
  6. Client money (will it be held?)
  7. Licensed bodies.
  8. Fees.
  9. Declaration.

  The reserved legal activities to be undertaken must also be disclosed. Section 7 deals specifically with ABS applicants and requires details of those with material interests in the entity (see below for more on what is a material interest) and those who otherwise have voting power and significant influence.

- FA2 – this must be completed by all non-lawyer managers, material interest holders, and the COLP and COFA, who need to be approved as suitable for these roles. The COLP must be a lawyer who is authorised to carry on reserved legal activities by an approved regulator. The COFA needs no specific qualifications but must be able to demonstrate a good working knowledge of the SRA Accounts Rules. For companies putting forward a finance director or accountant as their COFA this may require that individual to enrol on a course on the COFA role or the Accounts Rules if they have no previous experience of either. COLPs and COFAs are deemed approved under rule 13.5 of the Authorisation of Firms Rules in certain circumstances (see below).
- FA3 – this must be completed by a corporate owner or manager of the applicant.
- FA8 – the financial services notification form. The SRA is required to collect information for the Financial Conduct Authority about the financial services of the firms it regulates.
- FA10 – anti-money laundering form. The Money Laundering, Terrorist Financing and Transfer of Funds (Information on the Payer) Regulations 2017 (MLR) require the SRA to collect information about the firms it regulates.

As well as the forms, the SRA will also expect to receive as part of the application the following:

- a business plan (this is no longer mandatory but helps to explain key features of the business and can deal with compliance issues which the SRA may otherwise raise);
- projected turnover and cashflow for the first year of trading as an ABS;
- evidence of an offer of insurance from a participating insurer;
- the applicant's memorandum and articles of association; and
- the shareholders agreement.

The SRA will return in its entirety any application that is not complete and will require the applicant to re-submit it afresh. It is sensible, therefore, to check that all sections of the forms are fully filled in, including all boxes correctly ticked, and that all the accompanying documentation is attached before submission.

8.6 KEY REGULATORY AND LEGAL ISSUES LIKELY TO AFFECT AN ABS APPLICATION

Important issues which will, or are likely to, arise in connection with applications are set out below. Some will be covered to an extent by the FA1 application form but it can be helpful to explain how issues such as client confidentiality, conflicts of interest and separate businesses will be dealt with in the business plan, as this may preclude the need for the SRA to ask additional questions.

8.6.1 All material interests must be disclosed

One of the main issues for applicants is that of who and/or what body holds a 'material interest' in the applicant entity. It is important that these individuals/bodies are correctly identified in the application and that they are approved since it is an offence to fail to disclose a material interest.

LSA 2007, Sched.13 deals with the definition of a material interest. It is complicated but, in essence, is designed to identify anyone, or any body, who, or which, may have an influence over the way the ABS is run. The definition includes groupings, such as family members, who might act collectively and whose interests are aggregated to form a material interest. Those with material interests have to be measured against the requirements of the SRA Assessment of Character and Suitability Rules, which require full disclosure of criminal offences, disciplinary findings, financial conduct and other behaviour outlined in these rules. This is intended to ensure that only those who meet certain standards have power to control the provision of regulated legal services.

Essentially anyone who, or any body which, alone, or with associates, holds 10 per cent or more of the shares, voting rights or voting power in an ABS has a material interest. Similarly, if anyone or any body holds 10 per cent of the shares, voting rights or voting power in a parent undertaking of an ABS that is also classified as a material interest. 'Parent undertaking' has the same definition as in the Financial Services and Markets Act (FSMA) 2000.

This means, for example, that if a company holds 100 per cent of the shares in an ABS it will have a material interest which will need to be approved. Anyone or any entity holding a 10 per cent interest in that parent company will also need to be approved. Even if the company holds a minority of the shares in the ABS it might still be a parent undertaking if it has the power to exercise 'dominant influence' over it. Dominant influence could be, for example, that it refers a high percentage of work to the ABS.

Extensive guidance on material interests appears on the SRA's website in the guidance note on the ABS section called 'Does your interest in an ABS require SRA approval?' This can be found at **www.sra.org.uk/solicitors/guidance/ethics-guidance/does-your-interest-in-an-abs-require-sra-approval-**. The guidance emphasises, however, that it is the responsibility of the applicant to identify all material interests in its prospective ABS and that it is a matter of law on which the SRA will not give a ruling.

8.6.2 Appointment of the COLP and COFA

A Compliance Officer for Legal Practice (COLP) and a Compliance Officer for Finance and Administration (COFA) will need to be nominated and must be in place at all times (rule 8.1 of the SRA Authorisation of Firms Rules). COLPs and COFAs are not required for in-house legal teams where the employer is not an ABS.

Who can be a COLP or COFA and what these roles entail is set out in rule 8.2 of the SRA Authorisation of Firms Rules. An individual designated as a COLP and/or COFA must:

(a) be a *manager* or an *employee* of the *authorised body*;
(b) consent to the designation;
(c) not be disqualified from acting as a *HOLP* or *HOFA* under section 99 of the *LSA*; and
(d) in the case of a *COLP*, be an individual who is authorised to carry on *reserved legal activities* by an *approved regulator*.

COLPs and COFAs must be approved for these roles, although under rule 13.5 of the SRA Authorisation of Firms Rules an individual will be deemed approved if:

(a) that individual is a *lawyer* and a *manager* of the *authorised body*;
(b) the *authorised body* has an annual turnover of no more than £600,000;
(c) they are not a *compliance officer* of any other *authorised body*; and
(d) they are not subject to a regulatory or disciplinary investigation, or adverse finding or decision of the *SRA*, the *Tribunal* or another regulatory body.

Paragraph 9.1 of the SRA Code of Conduct for Firms requires a COLP to take all reasonable steps to ensure:

- compliance with the terms and conditions of their firm's authorisation;
- compliance by their firm and its managers, employees or owners with the SRA's regulatory arrangements;
- the managers and owners and those they employ and contract with do not cause or substantially contribute to any such breach;
- a prompt report is made to the SRA of any serious breach of the terms and conditions of their firm's authorisation or the SRA's regulatory arrangements.

Under paragraph 9.2, the COFA is responsible for taking reasonable steps to ensure:

- their firm and its managers and employees comply with the SRA Accounts Rules; and
- a prompt report is made of any breach of these rules.

It is clear that the SRA regards these roles as key to ensuring the businesses it regulates are properly managed and compliant with their regulatory obligations. They are regarded by the SRA not as titular roles but very much 'hands-on' roles. This means that the seniority of the individuals and their previous management experience will be carefully scrutinised.

The potential role holders will need to demonstrate, therefore, that they have the time to devote to the work required and also that they have sufficient seniority to exert influence over other employees and managers to ensure that compliance is treated seriously. Someone with just three years' post-qualification experience may struggle to get approval if they are being asked to direct others with greater seniority within the organisation. In relation to the COFA role it is essential that the candidate has experience of the Accounts Rules and not just general bookkeeping experience.

8.6.3 Separate business interests

The application form will ask about any separate business interests of the ABS and those of its owners and managers. A 'separate business' is defined in the SRA Glossary 2019; it is a business that is not an authorised legal services business but connected to one through common ownership or where there is a connection with both businesses through the activities of an individual.

For example, if an ABS (company Z) runs in common ownership and/or management with another unauthorised business (company Y), Y will be a separate business. This issue can have an influence on some applications and the SRA will want to be persuaded that clients will be clear about the loss of regulatory protections when they are referred to a separate business (i.e. from Z to Y). This will be particularly so if the companies operate within a group and with common branding. The Codes of Conduct for both individuals and firms require that where a client is referred or introduced to the separate business or a matter is to be split between the businesses, the client must give informed consent. These are issues that can usefully be explained in the applicant's business plan.

8.6.4 Client confidentiality and conflicts of interests

Other issues which the SRA will consider where Y wants to set up Z (an ABS) and run the two companies separately, are client confidentiality and conflicts of interest. The subject of confidentiality is particularly pertinent when the two businesses are to share office premises. The SRA will want to be assured that Z has separate lockable offices and that the computer systems of Z are separate and cannot be accessed by employees of Y. If any individuals are to be employed by both Y and Z, possible client conflicts will need to be identified and dealt with. Again, this could be covered in the business plan.

8.6.5 Referral fees

Where clients are referred to an ABS and referral fees are paid or some form of fee-sharing arrangement exists with the introducer, paragraph 5.1 of the Code for Individuals is relevant and clients must be made aware of the financial interest that the ABS has in the referral. The same applies if the ABS has a financial interest in referring clients to another party. A further consideration is the Legal Aid, Sentencing and Punishment of Offenders Act 2012 which prohibits payments for referrals in relation to personal injury claims. This is another area to be covered in the business plan so that the SRA can be clear about what clients will be told.

8.6.6 Once the application is submitted

The SRA usually confirms to all applicants within 24 hours that it has received all the documents it needs and that they have been correctly completed. After that, it conducts its due diligence in relation to all those bodies and individuals needing approval. A case handler looks in detail at the application in order to identify potential risk areas where further questions need to be raised. Once those have been satisfactorily dealt with, a start date from which the indemnity insurance can be effective is negotiated. The licence is then issued. Details of the new ABS, including its COLP and COFA, will appear on the SRA's ABS register which is open to the public. It is important to note that if there is any change in the circumstances of the application, these must be notified promptly to the SRA.

Finally, although the SRA does not usually ask to see any documents which will be part of the applicant's compliance plan or office manual, once the ABS starts to operate, appropriate policies, systems and procedures must be in place.

CHAPTER 9

Relevant legislation

9.1 INTRODUCTION

The SRA Code for Solicitors, RELs and RFLs (the Code for Individuals) contains many requirements which trigger a duty to keep up to date, and comply, with legislation. These apply to your own practice, whatever that might be, as well as your accountability for anyone you manage. For example:

> 3.2 You ensure that the service you provide to *clients* is competent and delivered in a timely manner.
>
> 3.3 You maintain your competence to carry out your role and keep your professional knowledge and skills up to date.
>
> 3.6 You ensure that the individuals you manage are competent to carry out their role, and keep their professional knowledge and skills, as well as understanding of their legal, ethical and regulatory obligations, up to date.
>
> 7.1 You keep up to date with and follow the law and regulation governing the way you work.

This means that all lawyers must identify the legislation that is relevant to them. There will be a significant overlap between the legislation which is relevant to lawyers working in-house and that which is relevant to those in private practice. However, because of the fact of their in-house status, the methods of compliance and the risks associated with breach of the legislation will be different for in-house lawyers.

In addition, and considering the personal duties bestowed on individual solicitors by the Code, there is a need to be clear about the managerial functions (however these might be described in the workplace) that would interest the SRA. Where an individual has any form of responsibility for others, it is important to be satisfied that this will include an appropriate element of control and influence over their training needs, etc.

This chapter identifies some of the key pieces of legislation which are relevant to in-house lawyers and which must be observed if they are going to demonstrate that these mandatory standards have been achieved. Bear in mind also that the legislation imposes personal duties on individuals as well as a number of corporate offences. The latter are of relevance to in-house lawyers with management responsibilities, who should consider the need for team training, systems and controls and due diligence of the risks. This is an example of the need to manage the risk of failure to comply with legislation for the business, and it requires clarity about the internal ownership of the risk and the role of the legal team. For example, what responsibility does the legal team have for the management of information security? Which department in the business takes ownership of risk management? What are the business's expectations of the legal team in terms of risk awareness, management and dealing with the aftermath of a security incident?

In addition to the legislation discussed in this chapter, there will also of course be specific pieces of legislation which must be observed in particular industries and because of the employer's business. For example the various Companies Acts, the Competition Act 1998 and the Enterprise Act 2002 will be important for those in commerce and industry; for those employed in local authorities, health and safety legislation, and the Local Government Acts and the Localism Act 2011 spring to mind.

Some legislation is likely to be relevant regardless of the specific type of in-house employment, and it is clear that there is a strong overlap with regulatory duties. The key pieces of legislation are those relating to anti-money laundering, counter terrorist finance and other frauds, financial services regulation, data protection, and equality legislation.

It goes without saying that money laundering and terrorist financing are two of the major global concerns of the twenty-first century. UK legislation is designed to be compatible with international safeguards and deterrents and to provide a network of information to combat such criminal activity.

9.2 PROCEEDS OF CRIME ACT 2002

The Proceeds of Crime Act (POCA) 2002 is designed principally with money laundering in mind. Money laundering can be described in the following way: it is the process by which the proceeds of crime, and the true ownership of those proceeds, are changed so that they have the appearance of coming from legitimate sources.

Everyone in the UK must comply with POCA 2002, in both a personal and professional capacity. In-house lawyers will need to be vigilant about this in terms of their employment, and with regard to the activities and behaviours of their employer, and, in cases where they act for third parties, those individuals as well.

The stages of money laundering are described as three connected processes: placement, layering and integration. First, cash generated from crime is placed in the financial system. Second, when the proceeds of crime are in the financial system, layering obscures their origins by passing the money through complex transactions. Third, when the origin of the funds has been obscured, the criminal is able to make the funds reappear as legitimate funds or assets.

The principal offences are set out in POCA 2002, ss.327–329 and are as follows:

- *Section 327 – concealing.* An offence is committed if a person conceals, disguises, converts, or transfers criminal property, or removes criminal property from England and Wales, Scotland or Northern Ireland. Concealing or disguising criminal property includes concealing or disguising its nature, source, location, disposition, movement, ownership or any rights connected with it.
- *Section 328 – arrangements.* An offence is committed if a person enters into, or becomes concerned in, an arrangement which they know or suspect facilitates the acquisition, retention, use or control of criminal property by or on behalf of another person.
- *Section 329 – acquisition, use or possession.* An offence is committed if a person acquires, uses or has possession of criminal property.

The penalties are draconian, with a maximum prison sentence of 14 years and/or a fine.

Solicitors in private practice have traditionally been easy targets for money launderers who are attracted to the endless possibilities which client accounts can give them to launder dirty money.

Money laundering risks for in-house lawyers are perhaps less obvious than for those in private practice but are no less real as a consequence. In-house lawyers will be less likely to operate client accounts and therefore cannot be used by criminals in that connection. However, perhaps more of a concern is the need for in-house lawyers to be alert to a number of ways in which their employer, or others to whom they are able to provide legal services, could be guilty of committing a criminal offence. Consider the following:

1. *Working in-house for a commercial organisation.* Do the tax arrangements of your employer suggest that evasion may be occurring or, perhaps, are you being asked to give tax and legal advice which is designed to facilitate tax evasion rather than more legitimate tax avoidance schemes?
2. *Working in-house in any type of organisation.* Is your employer choosing to disregard or not comply with legislation such as the Health and Safety Acts, so that any monies which would otherwise have legitimately been used for meeting mandatory health and safety requirements (insurances, etc.) could be regarded as criminal property?
3. *Working in-house but providing services to members of the public (such as in law centres and Citizens Advice).* Are you becoming aware of information about clients which suggests that they may be committing criminal acts such as not declaring income and receiving welfare benefits so that the latter may be regarded as criminal property?

All in-house lawyers should be alert to indicators of money laundering. In addition those in-house lawyers in managerial positions should ensure that team members also have knowledge of the concerns. There is an abundance of industry-specific guidance on warning signs, but more broadly the Legal Sector Affinity Group

Anti-Money Laundering Guidance for the Legal Sector contains a number of examples of what may amount to suspicious behaviour. This is available from the Law Society website along with a number of other useful resources for the legal profession (**www.lawsociety.org.uk**).

Examples of warning signs of suspicious behaviour include the following:

- secretive employer or third party client;
- being asked to do something outside your usual area of expertise;
- disputes which are settled too easily as this may indicate sham litigation;
- loss-making transactions where the loss is avoidable;
- dealing with money or property where you suspect that either is being transferred to avoid the attention of a trustee in a bankruptcy case, HMRC or a law enforcement agency;
- complex or unusually large transactions;
- unusual patterns of transactions which have no apparent economic purpose;
- concerns over source of funds; and
- transactions involving suspect territories.

Knowledge of any of the above may result in the individual lawyer being implicated in a money laundering offence with the double whammy of repercussions that this will create: first, a criminal offence under the legislation and, second, a regulatory offence because of the breach of the requirements in the SRA Standards and Regulations to comply with this legislation.

These are serious considerations and solicitors found to have assisted in money laundering offences have been prosecuted and disciplined. Take for example the case of Ross McKay. The report by John Hyde in the Law Society *Gazette* is shown below (*Gazette*, 8 January 2019).

'GO TO' SOLICITOR FOR DODGY PROPERTY DEALS JAILED FOR SEVEN YEARS

A conveyancing solicitor who fixed property deals for mortgage fraudsters has been jailed for seven years.

Ross McKay, 39, was sentenced at Manchester Crown Court last week after being found guilty of three offences of money laundering.

McKay provided conveyancing services to a criminal gang in order to launder money made from drug-dealing, tax evasion, and mortgage and property fraud, the court heard.

Deposits were put down on houses where the true, illegal source of the funds was disguised from the lenders; mortgage applications used nominees instead of the names of the legitimate purchasers; and claims about income were wildly exaggerated to secure loans.

McKay was responsible for more than 80 property transactions for various criminals, all of whom were subsequently convicted of offences including money laundering and fraud.

> Police said McKay, from Handforth in Cheshire, was the gang's 'go to' solicitor as they knew he would carry out property transactions without asking questions about the nature of their business, the sources of the deposits or the connections between parties in the transactions.
>
> Senior financial investigator Adrian Ladkin, of Greater Manchester Police's economic crime unit, said: 'McKay was fully aware that the purpose of the transactions was to launder criminal proceeds and he was deliberately dishonest in facilitating them. As a solicitor, McKay was in a position of trust, but he spectacularly failed in his legal duties through his corrupt and unlawful actions.'
>
> McKay's involvement was uncovered through Operation Isidor, an investigation run by the economic crime unit into the activities of criminal gang members.
>
> In sentencing, it has been reported that Judge Timothy Smith told McKay he was expected to act with the 'utmost integrity and honesty' in his role as a solicitor.
>
> 'In trial you portrayed yourself as being an average solicitor, one that helped to support your family but any outward show of professionalism was a charade,' said the judge. 'You allowed criminal property to be obtained and assisted these people in organised crime.'
>
> Last month, confiscation orders were obtained against defendants, including one who was ordered to pay £3.5m – the largest proceeds of crime case ever undertaken by Greater Manchester Police.
>
> McKay, admitted in 2004, is still listed on the roll as a non-practising solicitor. He will now be referred to the Solicitors Regulation Authority.

Neither the law nor the SRA distinguishes greatly between dishonesty and naivety as a cause of a breach of the legislation. It is therefore sensible that in-house lawyers take steps both to minimise personal risk and also to ensure that appropriate advice is given to their employer (and third party clients when permitted to act for them) of the risks of such breaches. By way of example, for in-house lawyers working in commerce and industry, it will be sensible to have, either implicitly or explicitly, a whistle-blowing policy and direct access to senior company officers so that any concerns can be discussed in an open and timely fashion. It may also be the case that the in-house lawyer will need to reach agreement about information which will be made available to them in order that they have sufficient knowledge with which to make the judgments about the business's activities and personal and corporate repercussions.

With in-house lawyers working as part of, or heading up, an in-house legal team, team training on the legislation is sensible due diligence as is, perhaps, the drawing up of a policy to facilitate disclosure of information which may be of concern. Where the in-house legal team provides services to members of the public, then training on the basic criminal activities in this area is sensible. At a minimum, lawyers and their teams should have an understanding of what constitutes criminal property, the meaning of suspicion (as established by *R* v. *da Silva* [2006] EWCA Crim 1654), an awareness of warning signs, and an appreciation that the business might sometimes need to make a suspicious activity report if it wants to ensure that it has a defence to an accusation of money laundering.

9.3 MONEY LAUNDERING REGULATIONS 2017 (AS AMENDED)

Everyone must comply with POCA 2002. This is not the case with the Money Laundering Regulations (MLR) 2017 (as amended) but assessment of its application is absolutely essential.

By way of introduction, MLR came into force in June 2017 replacing the Money Laundering Regulations 2007, SI 2007/2157. They were amended on 10 January 2020 through the implementation of the Fifth Money Laundering Directive as amended by the Money Laundering and Terrorist Financing (Amendment) Regulations 2019, SI 2019/1511. The MLR apply to those working in the 'regulated sector' on 'relevant business'.

The terms are defined in the following ways. The regulated sector is carrying on business in the UK in:

- credit institutions;
- financial institutions; and
- casinos;

and as:

- auditors;
- insolvency practitioners;
- external accountants and tax advisers;
- independent legal professionals;
- trust or company service providers;
- estate agents and letting agents;
- high value dealers;
- custodian wallet providers; and
- cryptoasset exchange providers.

An important point to note is that the definition of independent legal professional for the purposes of the regulated sector will only include a firm or a sole practitioner who by way of business provides legal or notarial services to other persons. It does not include solicitors working in-house simply by virtue of that fact alone.

In such a position a judgment must be made as to whether solicitors and their employers are required to comply with MLR because of the type of activities that they undertake; in other words whether they carry on relevant business.

It seems highly unlikely that solicitors working in law centres and other not-for-profit organisations will be bound to comply (this is a personal view and individuals employed in such an organisation will want to satisfy themselves on this point) but perhaps it is more likely that individuals working in commerce and industry or giving tax advice may be caught by the need to comply with MLR. The regulations only apply to certain activities – relevant business – where there is a high risk of money laundering. Examples include participation in financial or real property transactions concerning:

- buying and selling of real property or business entities;
- managing of client money, securities or other assets;
- opening or managing bank, savings or securities accounts;
- organisation of contributions necessary for the creation, operation or management of companies;
- creation, operation or management of trusts, companies or similar structures.

The purpose of MLR is to create an intelligence, reporting and auditing network so that national and international agencies can track money launderers and criminal property. In-house lawyers who are part of the relevant sector will want to ensure that they, and their employer, are able to comply with the duties imposed on them.

The key requirements are as follows:

1. Risk assessment – both at an organisational level and on individual matters.
2. Written policies, controls and procedures to mitigate and manage the money laundering and terrorist finance risks identified in the organisational risk assessment.
3. Appropriate internal controls – including the appointment of a member of the board (or equivalent) to be responsible for compliance and an independent audit function where appropriate with regard to the size and nature of the business.
4. Client due diligence (CDD) measures – or client identity checks. There is no requirement for an in-house lawyer to undertake CDD on their employer if the employer is the client in terms of the relevant business. However, if the lawyer, or the in-house legal team, as part of their employment provides services to third-party clients then CDD must be undertaken in respect of these clients. CDD is a risk response and there is the need to consider whether simplified due diligence might be appropriate.
5. Record-keeping.
6. The vetting and training of appropriate staff.
7. The appointment of a nominated officer known as the Money Laundering Reporting Officer (MLRO).

In many ways it would seem a natural choice for the in-house lawyer to be appointed as the business's MLRO. However, there are many personal implications in accepting this position, as the appointment does have possible legal, and in some cases regulatory, consequences for the role holder. As a lawyer, it is unwise for you to accept this position and consider that this is some kind of titular or token role only. Be aware of the implications of being the office holder and be satisfied that you have your employer's and the business's support for the task you have volunteered to undertake.

There is an important difference between compliance requirements for the purposes of POCA 2002 more generally and MLR more specifically in dealing with this position. Compliance with MLR means that the business must appoint a MLRO. Under POCA 2002 there is no such requirement, although some firms and businesses choose to do so on a voluntary, best practice basis, relating this to their risk strategies. However, a warning note comes with POCA 2002, s.332 and the failure to disclose offence which would be committed by anyone in this position regardless of whether this is a voluntary appointment under POCA 2002 or one required under MLR.

The following example of an enquiry undertaken by the FCA, and published on the FCA website (**www.fca.gov.uk**) will be of interest to anyone asked to consider accepting an appointment as a MLRO. The FCA's press release (dated 9 April 2019) is shown below.

FCA FINES STANDARD CHARTERED BANK £102.2 MILLION FOR POOR AML CONTROLS

The Financial Conduct Authority (FCA) has fined Standard Chartered Bank (Standard Chartered) £102,163,200 for Anti-Money Laundering (AML) breaches in two higher risk areas of its business. This is the second largest financial penalty for AML controls failings ever imposed by the FCA.

Today's announcement follows FCA investigations into two areas of Standard Chartered's business identified by the bank as higher risk: its UK Wholesale Bank Correspondent Banking business and its branches in the United Arab Emirates (UAE). The FCA found serious and sustained shortcomings in Standard Chartered's AML controls relating to customer due diligence and ongoing monitoring. Standard Chartered failed to establish and maintain risk-sensitive policies and procedures, and failed to ensure its UAE branches applied UK equivalent AML and counter-terrorist financing controls.

Under the Money Laundering Regulations 2007 (MLRs), Standard Chartered was required to establish and maintain appropriate and risk-sensitive policies and procedures to reduce the risk it may be used to launder the proceeds of crime, evade financial sanctions or finance terrorism. The MLRs also imposed a duty on Standard Chartered to require its global (non-EEA) branches and subsidiaries to apply policies and procedures in relation to due diligence and ongoing monitoring that are equivalent to those required of Standard Chartered in the UK.

The FCA found significant shortcomings in Standard Chartered's own internal assessments of the adequacy of its AML controls, its approach towards identifying and mitigating material money laundering risks and its escalation of money laundering risks. These failings exposed Standard Chartered to the risk of breaching sanctions and increased the risk of Standard Chartered receiving and/or laundering the proceeds of crime. Examples include:

- opening an account with 3 million UAE Dirham in cash in a suitcase (just over £500,000) with little evidence that the origin of the funds had been investigated;
- failing to collect sufficient information on a customer exporting a commercial product which could, potentially, have a military application. This product was exported to over 75 countries, including two jurisdictions where armed conflict was taking place or was likely to be taking place; and
- not reviewing due diligence on a customer despite repeated red flags such as a blocked transaction from another bank indicating a link to a sanctioned entity.

> Standard Chartered's failings occurred in its UK Correspondent Banking business during the period from November 2010 to July 2013 and in its UAE branches during the period from November 2009 to December 2014.
>
> Today, US authorities have also taken action against the Standard Chartered group for significant violations of US sanctions laws and regulations.
>
> Mark Steward, Director of Enforcement and Market Oversight at the FCA, said:
>
> 'Standard Chartered's oversight of its financial crime controls was narrow, slow and reactive. These breaches are especially serious because they occurred against a backdrop of heightened awareness within the broader, global community, as well as within the bank, and after receiving specific attention from the FCA, US agencies and other global bodies about these risks.
>
> Standard Chartered is working to improve its AML controls to ensure all issues are fully addressed on a global basis. The FCA has taken into account Standard Chartered's remediation work and its cooperation in assisting the FCA investigation, without which today's financial penalty would have been even higher.'
>
> The FCA has worked alongside a number of authorities during this investigation. Acknowledging the international co-operation in this case Mark Steward said:
>
> 'The FCA has worked closely and extensively with a number of UK and overseas agencies including the US Department of Justice, New York County District Attorney, US Board of Governors of the Federal Reserve, New York State Department of Financial Services and US Office of Foreign Assets Control. I would also like to acknowledge the assistance of the UAE Central Bank whose commitment has demonstrated the fight against money laundering is a truly global one, as it needs to be.'
>
> Standard Chartered did not dispute the FCA's findings and exercised its right, under the FCA's partly contested case process, to ask the FCA's Regulatory Decisions Committee to assess the appropriate level of sanction. Standard Chartered's agreement to accept the FCA's findings meant it qualified for a 30% discount. Otherwise, the FCA would have imposed a financial penalty of £145,947,500.

Offences include the following: failure to disclose offences under POCA 2002, ss.330 and 331 and the tipping-off offence under POCA 2002, s.333. Again, the penalties are severe: a maximum five-year prison sentence and/or a fine.

This means that any business for which money laundering may be a risk, regardless of whether or not it operates in the regulated sector, must have appropriate risk strategies to minimise the dangers of being implicated.

9.4 TERRORISM ACT 2000

While POCA 2002 and MLR are largely concerned with money laundering, the Terrorism Act 2000 is concerned with terrorist financing, i.e. making good money bad in order to support terrorist activities internationally or using bad money (criminal property) for the same reasons. So, terrorist financing can be described as monetary support for terrorist purposes.

This is another situation where in-house lawyers need to remain aware of their employer's activities. It goes without saying that it would be rare for a lawyer knowingly to work for an employer who supports and funds terrorism, but the ways in which in-house lawyers and their employers could be implicated in terrorism-related offences might include the following types of behaviour and warning signs:

- cash withdrawals being made from a business account not normally associated with cash transactions;
- telegraphic transfers made in small but repeated amounts;
- transactions involving foreign currency exchanges followed, within a short space of time, by transfers to suspect territories;
- opening bank accounts where funds arise in respect of suspect territories, behaviour, etc.; and
- dealing with funds or economic resources in a way which is intended to circumvent the financial restrictions on the transfer and use of terrorist funds.

Also, as with POCA 2002 issues, in-house lawyers providing services to members of the public will need to be vigilant about the knowledge which they may acquire.

Ways to mitigate the personal risks of being implicated in a terrorism offence are to include such considerations in the business's risk management strategy and, as appropriate, provide training to improve awareness and vigilance, direct access to the senior members of the business and the reassurance of an effective whistle-blowing policy.

9.5 CRIMINAL FINANCES ACT 2017

This has been a significant addition to the range of legislative responses to the issues arising in connection with money laundering, terrorist financing and fraud activities. It is relevant to all solicitors regardless of the type of business in which they are employed.

The Act has created a criminal offence for any entity that does not prevent the criminal facilitation of tax evasion by associated persons, whether this is UK tax evasion or the evasion of foreign tax. The offence has been introduced in order to prosecute professional firms and other bodies that fail to take steps to stop associated persons criminally facilitating tax evasion.

The employing organisation will be expected to demonstrate a clear commitment to compliance, top level commitment to the risks, communication of expectations internally, and to adopt an implementation plan to ensure an appropriate response. There are corporate liability offences which must be considered. There is one statutory defence only and that is where the firm has in place reasonable prevention procedures or is able to show that it was reasonable not to have had such procedures in place.

Working in an in-house legal role, it is important to be confident that the organisation is aware of the issues, has identified high-risk areas of its operation, and has appropriate processes and training.

9.6 FINANCIAL SERVICES AND MARKETS ACT 2000

Financial services make a significant contribution to the UK economy. Over one million people are employed in the financial services industry and the UK is the world's leading exporter of financial services. In 2009, 10 per cent of the UK's total economic output was from this sector.

It is a heavily regulated industry, for a number of reasons. The Barlow Clowes, Bank of Credit and Commerce and Robert Maxwell pensions scandals occurred in an era of lighter, self-regulation. The more onerous regulatory obligations which are now in place are intended to demonstrate that such events should now be difficult to repeat and that this is a trusted industry with a good reputation.

The Financial Services and Markets Act (FSMA) 2000 is the key piece of legislation in this area. It makes the Financial Conduct Authority (FCA) and the Prudential Regulation Authority (PRA) statutory regulators of financial services in the UK and creates the general prohibition in s.19 which states:

> (1) No person may carry on a regulated activity in the United Kingdom, or purport to do so, unless he is –
>
> (a) an authorised person; or
> (b) an exempt person.

It is an offence to carry on regulated activities in breach of this prohibition. The penalties are in FSMA 2000, s.23; it may be a criminal offence and punishable on indictment by a maximum term of two years' imprisonment and/or a fine. Section 26 states that any contract entered into in breach of the general prohibition is unenforceable.

Solicitors working in law firms which are authorised and regulated by the SRA are able to rely on the Part XX exemption in FSMA 2000 (provision of financial services by members of the professions) to avoid breaching the general prohibition. Because the Law Society is a designated professional body, and because the SRA has made rules to regulate the scope of the regulated activities which law firms may undertake (i.e. the Financial Services (Scope) Rules which are in the SRA Standards and Regulations section of the SRA website), the majority of law firms do not need to be authorised by the SRA and can nevertheless undertake a number of financial services for their clients as part of their professional services.

In-house lawyers do not work in businesses which are authorised and regulated by the SRA and it is essential that they understand that they cannot rely on the Part XX exemption. Some in-house lawyers working in commerce and industry will very clearly be working in financial services businesses, such as banks, building societies and insurance companies, and the authorisation position will be well established. They should be familiar with the regulatory requirements of the FCA and the compliance requirements that this creates for both them and their employer and which are contained in the FCA Handbook.

The position may not be so clear-cut for in-house lawyers who are working in smaller commercial companies. They will need to undertake the following analysis of their position and that of their employer:

- Are we carrying on regulated activities in the course of business?
- Do we need to be authorised by the FCA or can we rely on any exclusions or other exemptions to avoid this requirement?

The meaning of 'regulated activity' is defined in FSMA 2000, s.22(1):

> An activity is a regulated activity for the purposes of this Act if it is an activity of a specified kind which is carried on by way of business and:
>
> (a) relates to an investment of a specified kind; or
> (b) in the case of an activity of a kind which is also specified for the purposes of this paragraph, is carried on in relation to property of any kind.

Regulated activities and investments are listed in secondary legislation known as the Financial Services and Markets Act (Regulated Activities) Order (RAO) 2001, SI 2001/544. Common regulated investments and common regulated activities are shown below.

Common regulated investments are:

- deposits;
- electronic money;
- contracts of insurance;
- instruments creating or acknowledging indebtedness;
- shares;
- sukuk (shariah-compliant debt instruments);
- government and public securities;
- units in a collective investment scheme;
- rights under a stakeholder pension scheme or a personal pension scheme;
- options;
- futures;
- regulated mortgage contracts;
- Lloyd's syndicate capacity and syndicate membership;
- rights under funeral plan contracts;
- home reversion plans;
- regulated sale and rent back agreements;
- credit-related regulated agreements.

Common regulated activities are:

- accepting deposits;
- issuing e-money;

- effecting or carrying out contracts of insurance as principal;
- dealing in investments (as principal or agent);
- arranging deals in investments;
- managing investments;
- assisting in the administration and performance of a contract of insurance;
- sending dematerialised instructions;
- establishing, etc. collective investment schemes;
- advising on investments;
- advising on, arranging, entering into and administering home finance activities;
- Lloyd's market activities;
- arranging a regulated credit agreement.

Identifying investments and activities is relatively straightforward. The more difficult judgment is whether the regulated activity is being carried on by way of business. The FCA gives guidance on this in the FCA Handbook in the Perimeter Guidance manual section 14.5. Although this guidance arises in respect of a particular regulated activity (specifically home reversion activities), it is a useful indicator of the FCA's views, as it states the business test requires the following analysis:

- the degree of continuity;
- the existence of a commercial element;
- the scale of the activity;
- the proportion which the activity bears to other activities carried on by the same person but which are not regulated; and
- the nature of the particular regulated activity that is carried on.

The case of *Smith* v. *Anderson* (1880) 15 Ch 247 is often quoted in this context. In this case, business for the purpose of the matters under consideration was defined as 'a series of acts which, if successful, would obtain a gain'.

Making an accurate analysis is vital given the offences attached to breaching the general prohibition. In-house lawyers carrying on regulated activities for either their employer or permitted third parties will need to consider their position most carefully. If they make the judgment that they are carrying on regulated activities in the course of their employment then the employer will need to obtain authorisation from the FCA and comply with the relevant sections of the FCA Handbook.

There are only two alternatives to authorisation: either to avoid carrying on regulated activities or be satisfied that an exclusion can be used.

RAO 2001 contains both regulated activities and regulated investments. It also includes a number of exclusions: broadly, scenarios or conditions in which what would seemingly be a regulated activity is statutorily excluded but in the very strict control conditions that all conditions attached to the exclusion can be met.

The practical implication is that reliance on an exclusion means that the business is not carrying on a regulated activity and does not need to comply with FSMA 2000 and the Part XX exemption in the case of professional firms, or the FCA Handbook in respect of non-exempt firms. The danger is that a misinterpretation of the conditions pertaining to the exclusion is likely to mean that the business breaches the general prohibition and commits an offence under FSMA 2000.

Exclusions which may be of benefit to in-house lawyers are described in Table 9.1 (adapted from a table originally published by the SRA).

Another regulated activity which in-house lawyers must be wary of is the making of a financial promotion. FSMA 2000, s.21 contains a restriction on financial promotions in that unauthorised persons cannot, in the course of business, communicate an invitation or inducement to engage in investment activity, unless it has been approved by an authorised person.

This prohibition is enforced by the criminal offence in FSMA 2000, s.25 of making an unauthorised financial promotion. Because of the professional (and personal) consequences of a criminal conviction, an in-house lawyer working in a business which is not itself authorised must take care not to make a financial promotion.

A financial promotion may be made in several ways and it is important to understand terminology such as 'real time' and 'non-real time', 'solicited' and 'unsolicited communications' and understand the requirements of the secondary legislation which is relevant, namely the Financial Services and Markets Act 2000 (Financial Promotion) Order 2005, SI 2005/1529 (FPO 2005) which amended the Financial Promotion Order 2001.

A 'real time communication' is described in art.7(1) as 'a personal visit, telephone conversation or other interactive dialogue'. Anything else is 'non-real time', e.g. investment information communicated via a letter, fax, email, advertisement, brochure or website (in broad terms, anything in writing).

Real time communications are further subdivided into 'solicited' and 'unsolicited'. If the investment business discussion is initiated by the other person (e.g. the employer or the client) in a meeting with the in-house lawyer then the communication is 'solicited'. If the issue is raised for the first time by the lawyer, then it is 'unsolicited'.

Because of the risks attached with improper and inappropriate financial promotions, the making of them is heavily regulated so that they must be made by an authorised firm. If an in-house lawyer's employer is authorised, then the in-house lawyer, and indeed other employees, will be entitled to make financial promotions.

However, there are some exemptions in FPO 2005 which allow unauthorised firms to make promotions. Those which are likely to be of use to in-house lawyers are listed in Table 9.2 (adapted from a table originally published by the SRA) but as with the exclusions from regulated activities described in the preceding paragraphs, great caution should be exercised when using these exemptions.

Table 9.1 Exclusions included in the Financial Services and Markets Act (Regulated Activities) Order 2001 that may be of benefit to in-house lawyers

Exclusion	What you can do	Conditions
Using an authorised person – RAO 2001, arts.22 and 29	Deal as agent or arrange a transaction with or through an authorised person where the transaction is entered into on the advice of the authorised person or it is clear that the client has not sought your advice as to the merits of the transaction.	(1) Cannot be used where the specified investment is a contract of insurance. (2) You must account to the client for any commission you receive.
Arrangements not causing a deal – RAO 2001, art.26	Excludes from the regulated activity of arranging in respect of securities and regulated mortgage contracts any arrangements which do not bring about the transaction to which it relates.	None, but remember the need to achieve the standards in paragraphs 8.1, 8.2–8.5 and 8.6–8.11 of the Code for Individuals when offering services to clients.
Introducing – RAO 2001, art.33	Introduce a client to an authorised person for independent advice.	(1) Cannot be used where the specified investment is a contract of insurance. (2) Arrangements must not go beyond introductions.
Introducing – RAO 2001, art.33A	Introduce a client to an authorised person to arrange and/or advise on a regulated mortgage contract.	(1) You must not receive any money paid by the client for or in connection with any transaction that the client enters into with the authorised person. (2) Before making the introduction you must disclose to the client details of any commission, etc. you receive for the introduction. (3) Remember the need to achieve the standards in paragraphs 8.1, 8.2–8.5 and 8.6–8.11 of the SRA Code.

Exclusion	What you can do	Conditions
Trustees, nominees and personal representatives – RAO 2001, art.66	Applicable to lawyers who are acting as trustees, nominees and personal representatives and allows them to arrange, deal, manage investments, safeguard and administer, send dematerialised instructions, and advise.	(1) Cannot be used where the specified investment is a contract of insurance. (2) The solicitor trustee, nominee or personal representative must not receive remuneration for carrying on the regulated activity in addition to the remuneration obtained for providing the trustee, etc. service. (3) The advising regulated activity is limited to advice to a fellow trustee. (4) For the dealing, managing and safeguarding and administrating regulated activities, trustees must not hold themselves out as providing such a service.
The necessary exclusion – RAO 2001, art.67	Exclusion applies to regulated activities of dealing and arranging safe custody and assets and applies where the regulated activity may reasonably be regarded as a necessary part of other services provided in the course of that business.	(1) Cannot be used where the specified investment is a contract of insurance. (2) The regulated activity must not be separately remunerated from the professional services.

Exclusion	What you can do	Conditions
Sale/purchase of a company – RAO 2001, art.70	Exclusion applies to the regulated activities of dealing as principal or agent, arranging deals and giving advice in connection with the purchase or sale of shares in a company other than an open ended investment company.	(1) The shares consist of/include 50 per cent plus of the voting shares in the company OR the shares together with any shares already held by the purchaser consist of 50 per cent plus of the voting shares AND each of the parties to the sale/purchase is either a company, a partnership, a single individual or a group of connected individuals. (2) If condition in (1) cannot be met, the solicitor can still act where the object of the transaction can reasonably be regarded as the acquisition of day-to-day control of the company's affairs.
Provision of information on an incidental basis – RAO 2001, art.72C	Excludes from the activities of arranging and assisting in the performance of a contract of insurance, the provision of information to a policyholder or potential policyholder.	Must reasonably be regarded as being incidental to the solicitor's business.

Table 9.2 Exclusions included in the Financial Services and Markets Act 2000 (Financial Promotions) Order 2005 that may be of benefit to in-house lawyers

Exemption	Permitted financial promotion	Conditions
One-off non-real time communications and solicited real time communications – FPO 2001, art.28	Allows individuals to make a one-off financial promotion, e.g. by letter addressed to a specific client or during a meeting with a particular client.	The communication must be made to one recipient, or a group of recipients acting together. The investment concerned must have been identified having regard to the particular circumstances of the client. The communication must not be part of an organised marketing campaign.
One-off unsolicited real time communications – FPO 2001, art.28A	Allows individual to make a one-off financial promotion to a client during a meeting or by telephone, etc.	As in art.28, plus: • The individual believes on reasonable grounds that the client understands the risks of engaging in the investment activity to which the promotion relates. • The client must have been expecting the individual to contact them.
Introductions – FPO 2001, art.15	Allows an individual to promote the fact that they can make an introduction to an authorised person with a view to the provision of independent financial advice.	The individual must account to the client for any commission it receives. The authorised person cannot be associated with the firm.

9.7 EQUALITY ACT 2010

Solicitors have always been under a very strict conduct duty not to unlawfully discriminate in their dealings with clients and third parties and handling equality issues correctly is a non-negotiable requirement.

The regulatory objectives in LSA 2007 make this clear with such requirements as approved regulators having the mandate to improve access to justice, protect and promote the interests of consumers and to encourage an independent, strong, diverse and effective legal profession (see s.1).

These requirements run alongside the equalities legislation and are now made clear in SRA principle 6 (the duty that you act in a way that encourages equality, diversity and inclusion) and by paragraph 1.1 of the Code for Individuals (the duty that you do not unfairly discriminate by allowing your personal views to affect your professional relationships and the way in which you provide your services).

Failure to comply with the relevant parts of the SRA Standards and Regulations can have serious consequences, not only in terms of disciplinary issues but also because of the legal ramifications and consequent reputational issues. There are some very visible cases in the public domain where law firms and lawyers have misjudged their duties. These cases will carry the same message for in-house lawyers about the consequences of breaching the legislation:

- *Bivonas LLP & Others* v. *Bennett* (UKEAT/0254/11/JOJ) – unlawful discrimination against an employee on the grounds of sexual orientation.
- *Osborne Clarke Services* v. *Purohit* (UKEAT/0305/08/JOJ) – a failure to consider job applications from non-EEA nationals was indirect racial discrimination.
- *Eversheds Legal Services Ltd* v. *De Belin* (UKEAT/0352/10/JOJ) – unlawful sexual discrimination.

Achieving compliance promotes a number of benefits in creating the right ethos in the workplace: the ideal will be that everyone treats colleagues, clients and third parties with respect. Also, a strong culture of equality and diversity is a selling point when tendering for business and in demonstrating adherence to various quality standards.

Until 2010, legislative duties were found in countless different statutes (for example, the Sex Discrimination Act 1975 and the Race Relations Act 1976). These were consolidated in the Equality Act 2010.

This legislation identifies nine protected characteristics which are as follows:

- age;
- disability;
- gender reassignment;
- marriage and civil partnership;
- pregnancy and maternity;
- race;
- religion or belief;
- sex; and
- sexual orientation;

and makes it an offence to unlawfully discriminate (either directly or indirectly), victimise or harass someone on the grounds of a protected characteristic.

Consider the following:

1. Are you satisfied that your organisation's working practices comply with the legislation?
2. Have you assessed your organisation's practices, etc. and are you satisfied that compliance with these does not place you in difficulties with regulatory expectations?

3. Do you make reasonable adjustments to ensure that clients and employees with disabilities are treated in the same way as their counterparts who are not disabled?
4. Are you confident that victimisation and/or harassment is not tolerated and would be challenged as inappropriate behaviour?

In many ways, in-house lawyers may be in more informed positions about equality matters than their private practice counterparts. Commercial organisations, and public authorities, have long been forerunners in accommodating flexible working, having transparent policies for recruitment, development and promotion opportunities, and for seeing the need to demonstrate to clients that they treat people with respect. The challenge for in-house lawyers would be to be satisfied that the organisation is meeting the requirements of legislation and that they personally can reconcile their duties to their employer with the law and their personal regulatory requirements.

9.8 BRIBERY ACT 2010

The Bribery Act 2010 came into force in July 2011. It is intended to be a deterrent to improper behaviour as much in the public sector as in the private sector, and applies to all dealings wherever these may take place in the world. As a consequence it is of great significance to all lawyers regardless of their type of employment.

Under the Act it is an offence for a UK citizen or resident to pay or receive a bribe, either directly or indirectly. Companies and partnerships can commit an offence if a bribe is paid on their behalf by an 'associate' (meaning employees, agents, or anyone else providing services on their behalf). The corporate defence to this offence is to have adequate procedures in place to prevent the action occurring.

The penalties are unlimited company fines, up to 10 years' imprisonment for individuals and debarment from tendering for public contracts in the European Union.

As yet, there are very few examples of prosecutions although the first conviction did arise in a legal environment when a magistrates' court administrative officer admitted taking a £500 bribe to 'get rid' of a speeding charge. The individual in question was sentenced to six years' imprisonment at Southwark Crown Court in November 2011 which was reduced to four years on appeal (*R* v. *Patel (Munir Yakub)* [2012] EWCA Crim 1243).

The Bribery Act is relevant to all types of in-house lawyers who will want to be satisfied on certain key points – essentially that there is an awareness of the legislation and that the senior directors, managers, etc. are committed to ensuring that there are no breaches. Avoidance measures may include:

- a risk analysis of the business;
- adequate training of key personnel;
- an adequate whistle-blowing policy;

- an anti-bribery policy; and
- direct access to key members of the organisation.

Much of the risk strategy is likely to be linked to the business's systems and controls to deal with money laundering and other fraudulent activities.

The anti-bribery policy need not be overly complicated. Guidance issued by the Ministry of Justice (**www.justice.gov.uk/guidance/docs/bribery-act-2010-guidance.pdf**) includes suggestions about the procedures which commercial organisations can put into place to prevent persons associated with them from committing acts of bribery. The guidance makes the following point:

> The objective of the Act is not to bring the full force of the criminal law to bear upon well-run commercial organisations that experience an isolated incident of bribery on their behalf.

With this in mind, the guidance contains six management principles which are as follows:

- proportionate procedures;
- top level commitment;
- risk assessment;
- due diligence;
- communication; and
- monitoring and review.

Bearing these principles in mind, there are many similarities with SRA governance requirements with the focus on corporate governance and responsibility, an entity-based compliance culture, training, monitoring and review.

The organisation's anti-bribery policy should therefore take into account the particular risks of the particular business. Some questions to address include:

- Do you use intermediaries?
- Do you do business in high-risk countries?
- Do you do business with government?
- Do you have other interactions with government?
- Does your policy make it clear what your position and expectations are?
- Does it have processes to check associates?
- Do you have a policy on gifts and entertainment?
- What record-keeping requirements will there be?
- Will there be training of all staff?
- What systems will be implemented to monitor and review?

It is unlikely that legitimate referral fees and reasonable and proportionate hospitality will be caught by the Act. Again, the Ministry of Justice makes this point:

> The government does not intend for the Act to prohibit reasonable and proportionate hospitality and promotional or other similar business expenditure intended for these purposes.

For reasons similar to those associated with money laundering legislation, it seems likely that a business will look to the in-house lawyer to advise on the type of bribery policy which would be appropriate for its needs. As with money laundering risks, the in-house lawyer will be well advised to ensure that everyone within the organisation has the appropriate awareness of both the legislation and the business's tolerance levels. Training is advisable, as is the maintenance of appropriate record-keeping to document examples of gifts and hospitality, etc. Access to senior levels of the business, and a whistle-blowing policy, may also guard against ignorance of breaches.

9.9 GENERAL DATA PROTECTION REGULATION AND THE DATA PROTECTION ACT 2018

The General Data Protection Regulation (GDPR) and the Data Protection Act 2018 came into force in the UK on 25 May 2018 replacing the Data Protection Act 1998.

The management of information security is a regulatory risk priority and it is likely to be identified as a commercial risk issue in the organisation which employs the in-house lawyer. Data incidents are likely to have legal and business implications as well as the ability to create adverse publicity and reputational damage. For regulated individuals within the organisation, such as solicitors, their role in the business's response could create regulatory and disciplinary issues for them.

All organisations will be processing data and it is essential that there is an appropriate response to the issue. For example, as a lawyer in the business, it is sensible to ensure that the following actions are undertaken:

- data processing activities have been identified;
- data subjects have also been identified;
- the legal grounds for data processing have been established;
- there is compliance with the data protection principles in the GDPR;
- relevant information has been given to data subjects;
- there are appropriate policies to deal with the storage, retention and destruction of personal data;
- data breach prevention and risk management measures are in place;
- there is a subject access request process;
- adequate training is provided to all relevant staff; and
- the organisation's response is monitored for continuing effectiveness and appropriateness.

The headlines connected with GDPR have largely focused on the considerable increase in fining powers. The Information Commissioner's Office has the power to impose fines of up to €20 million, and some organisations which employ in-house lawyers may be processing such quantities of data that would mean that the threat of this level of fine must be managed.

However, this is at the far end of the scale and most issues will result in lesser monetary fines but nevertheless there are the same risks associated with scrutiny and reputational damage. Consider the following examples where lawyers and others were subject to censure under the Data Protection Act 1998:

- Stoke on Trent City Council fined £120,000 after an in-house solicitor sent highly sensitive information about a child protection matter to the wrong email address.
- Oxfordshire County Council had to sign an undertaking to keep data safe and secure after an in-house solicitor dropped sensitive data in child protection matters about 22 individuals in the street.
- James Pickles, who previously worked at Jordans Solicitors in Dewsbury, Yorkshire, was prosecuted for illegally taking information about more than 100 people before leaving for a rival firm. The information was contained in six emails sent by Pickles in the weeks before he left Jordans.
- CPS fined £200,000 in respect of laptops containing unencrypted data which had been stolen, even though the data had not been read.

CHAPTER 10

Accreditation schemes

Increasingly, third parties are using accreditation schemes as shortcuts to make judgments about the service provider they are using.

Lawyers can use such schemes to demonstrate their skills in two ways: first, in an individual capacity to prove the standard of competence which they have personally attained in a particular area of work and, second, in terms of their business, to demonstrate that their workplace meets prescribed standards in terms of compliance and quality.

The benefits of accreditation are numerous. It can:

- provide a recognisable acknowledgment of attainment of skills;
- facilitate the promotion of good practice within a business;
- enable consistency of approach within the business;
- create implicit advertising of values and quality;
- provide assurances to the public;
- possibly provide a competitive edge when tendering for contracts, etc.;
- provide assurances to regulators, insurers and others;
- enable the individual and the business to demonstrate their strengths.

This chapter looks at the schemes which are of relevance to in-house lawyers: specifically, the various accreditation schemes administered by both the Law Society and the SRA which are relevant to individual lawyers regardless of where they are employed, and also the schemes which are available to in-house legal teams such as Lexcel, the Specialist Quality Mark and the ISO 9001 standards. Some of these are mandatory requirements while others are 'nice to have' bolt-ons.

10.1 PERSONAL ACCREDITATION

Accreditation of individual solicitors is awarded by the Law Society and the SRA.

The Law Society schemes are broadly voluntary in nature although for some types of Legal Aid Agency contracts it will be necessary to show that some individuals within the organisation have such accreditation.

The SRA schemes are mandatory requirements in certain areas of law.

All such accreditation focuses on achievement of particular standards in relation to areas of law.

The following gives information about schemes which may be of interest to in-house lawyers.

10.1.1 Children Law Accreditation Scheme

Who can apply

Solicitors and Chartered Institute of Legal Executives (CILEx) members, including those working for local authorities, who have completed a compulsory training course with an approved provider before making an application.

There are two categories of membership: private practitioner and local authority membership.

Accreditation criteria – key points

Covers all types of public law children work.

With local authority membership, it is necessary to show experience of representing local authorities in public law proceedings under the Children Act 1989 and other family proceedings as defined in the Act. CILEx applicants who are employed by local authorities must demonstrate that they are authorised by their employer under the Local Government Act 1972, s.223.

Entry to the scheme is by independent assessment of case reports and possibly by interview. Applicants will be required to demonstrate that they are fit and proper and must obtain an enhanced Disclosure and Barring Service (DBS) disclosure. Standards of competence must be demonstrated by reference to various statutory and ethical duties and by continuing professional development studies. All members agree to follow the Law Society Code of Practice for Children Law.

Duration of accreditation

Membership lasts for five years and members can reapply by completing the re-accreditation process.

10.1.2 Criminal Litigation Accreditation Scheme

Who can apply

Solicitors, CILEx members and registered European lawyers who are registered with the SRA.

Accreditation criteria – key points

Designed to allow individuals to qualify to apply for inclusion on local duty solicitor rotas under the Legal Services Commission's Criminal Defence Service Duty Solicitor Arrangements 2001.

There are three stages to attaining membership:

- passing the Police Station Qualification (PSQ);
- passing the Magistrates Court Qualification (MCQ); and
- meeting the fitness and propriety standards.

The award of the PSQ and MCQ is by way of assessment, submission of portfolios and role-play tests. Standards of competence are prescribed by reference to legislation, practice and ethical duties.

Duration of accreditation

Membership is for an initial term of five years. See the Law Society website for details of the re-accreditation process.

10.1.3 Immigration and Asylum Law Accreditation Scheme

Who can apply

Solicitors and CILEx members. Non-solicitor employees employed in a law firm or a business regulated by the Office of the Immigration Services Commissioner (OISC) can also apply. Membership of the scheme is compulsory for immigration lawyers working under the immigration and asylum category of a Legal Aid Agency (LAA) contract (such as lawyers in Citizens Advice and law centres providing such services).

Accreditation criteria – key points

There are different levels of membership with the various levels assessed by reference to competency standards (by various methods including multiple choice, examinations, drafting skills, mock client interview, etc.) and with the requirement to have knowledge of legislation, practice and professional skills.

Duration of accreditation

Application for re-accreditation must be made before the expiry of membership of the scheme and details are available on the Law Society website.

10.1.4 Immigration Law Advanced Accreditation Scheme

Who can apply

Level 2 caseworkers under the Immigration Law Accreditation Scheme can apply for advanced accreditation.

Accreditation criteria – key points

A higher level of understanding of immigration and asylum law is required. Demonstration of the successful management of complex cases, sharing expertise and influencing the development of law, policy and practice with credibility, if not success, is required. Assessment is by way of a Selection Panel and the passing of a fitness and propriety test. There is a requirement to complete continuing professional development (CPD) studies in relevant topics.

Duration of accreditation

Details of the re-accreditation requirements can be found on the Law Society website.

10.1.5 Mental Health Act Scheme

Who can apply

Solicitors and members of CILEx can apply for membership after they have undertaken training with an approved course provider.

In-house lawyers working in law centres may find this of relevance.

Accreditation criteria – key points

Relates to the representation of patients in all proceedings before the First-tier Tribunal (Mental Health) under the Mental Health Act 1983. Application can be made after completion of compulsory training and applicants must also submit evidence of representation or observing various types of hearings, case reports and other information as required. All applicants must also submit an enhanced DBS disclosure. Assessment is by interview. Members must agree to follow the Law Society's Code of Practice for Mental Health and undertake CPD training to keep knowledge up to date.

Duration of accreditation

Initial re-accreditation is after three years and thereafter at five-year intervals. There is the need to demonstrate continued competence in the area of law.

10.1.6 Other schemes

Other personal accreditation schemes are unlikely to be of interest to in-house lawyers but it is worth noting what they are and the fact that they are open to all solicitors who can meet the membership criteria:

- Civil and Commercial Mediation – the Law Society;
- Clinical Negligence – the Law Society;
- Family Law – the Law Society;
- Family Law Advanced – the Law Society;
- Family Mediation – the Law Society;
- Personal Injury – the Law Society;
- Planning Law – the Law Society;
- Police Station Representatives Accreditation Scheme (for non-solicitor employees) – the SRA.

10.2 ACCREDITATION OF THE TEAM OR THE BUSINESS

Law firms in private practice and in-house legal teams are also able to apply for accreditation of their business. Sometimes this is a mandatory requirement, such as for those organisations which have an LAA contract, and sometimes it is as a voluntary accreditation used as means of achieving and demonstrating service and quality values.

The schemes which are particularly beneficial to in-house legal teams are described below.

10.2.1 Lexcel

Lexcel is the Law Society's own practice management quality mark which can be obtained by any type of practice, whether this is private practice or an in-house legal team. It is not compulsory but there are benefits in obtaining accreditation in that it ensures that businesses have a means of demonstrating service excellence both internally to staff and employers and externally to insurers, regulators and to clients seeking that they participate in beauty parades. It is also a way of demonstrating achievement of the rules, regulations and standards in the SRA Standards and Regulations. It is increasing in popularity.

Lexcel is an independently assessed scheme and there are a number of policies, plans and procedures which businesses must adopt to demonstrate compliance. The current version is Lexcel v6.1, which launched in 2018 and is the compulsory version for any firm or in-house legal team seeking initial accreditation since then.

The in-house guide is reproduced in full in **Appendix B**.

10.2.2 Specialist Quality Mark

Some law firms and not-for-profit organisations provide information, advice and legal representation to members of the public with the benefit of public funding. Such organisations are awarded contracts by the LAA to provide services in this manner, and must hold a Quality Mark, or alternatively Lexcel accreditation, to undertake legal work under the contract.

The Quality Mark is a suite of three different quality assurance standards: the Specialist Quality Mark (SQM), the Family Mediation Quality Mark (MQM) and the Quality Mark for the Bar (QMB).

The SQM is of particular relevance to in-house legal teams in this area. These are likely to be in-house legal teams working in law centres or for charitable institutions that provide legal support to members of the public. It was introduced in 2002 and is principally intended to ensure that organisations can demonstrate that they are well managed, with good client care and that they have appropriate systems to ensure that good quality advice is provided to their clients.

Auditing occurs before a contract is awarded and at regular periods thereafter when the organisation is applying to renew its contract. The auditing is currently undertaken by an independent commercial organisation, the SQM Delivery Partnership, on behalf of the LAA.

Auditing is undertaken with reference to the Specialist Quality Mark Standard which focuses on assessing quality, practice, etc. in seven key areas (Specialist Quality Mark Standard 2012, paragraph 1.3):

- Access to Service – planning the service, making others aware of the service and non-discrimination.
- Seamless Service – signposting and referral to other agencies.
- Running the Organisation: the roles and responsibilities of key staff, and financial management.
- People Management – equal opportunities for staff, training and development, supervision and supervisors' standards.
- Running the Service – case management, independent review of files and feedback to caseworkers.
- Meeting Clients' Needs – providing information to clients, confidentiality, privacy and fair treatment, and maintaining quality where someone else delivers part of the service.
- Commitment to Quality – complaints, other user feedback and maintaining quality procedures.

Compliance with the Specialist Quality Mark Standard is mandatory and is intended to demonstrate to the LAA, as the funding agent, and to clients and the public more generally, that the business supports and fulfils key values. These values are described in the following ways:

- Improved risk management techniques – for example, the need to demonstrate conflict checking and proper supervision.

- Improved client care – for example, the requirement to demonstrate to the LAA that clients are given information about service and cost implications both at the outset and at regular intervals during the retainer.
- Effective management practices – with the intention of demonstrating a well-run business with appropriate costs supported by business plans, financial sense, and effective governance.
- Effective use of staff – with evidence on training and adequate supervision to ensure that the business's resources are appropriately used.
- Increased client confidence.
- LAA confidence that the business is providing services to a minimum standard which is an appropriate standard.

A contract is usually awarded for a three-year period. The independent auditors use a mixture of desk-based, remote assessment and attendance at the business address to undertake file reviews, interview staff and generally check that systems and procedures are being used. Most audits result in the business being awarded a pass/continue/continue with corrective action certificate with time limits being imposed for demonstration that the corrective actions have been completed.

10.2.3 ISO 9001

The International Organization for Standardization (ISO) is an international organisation that creates global quality standards which are currently being used by over one million different types of services worldwide. ISO data shows that the UK businesses which have achieved this quality standard include lawyers in both private practice and in-house legal teams in the employed sector (**www.iso.org**).

The ISO 9001 is a suite of quality management standards which is intended to demonstrate that a business's products or services meet the customer's or client's requirements and that there is a focus on improving quality standards. The ISO 9001 provides the quality management specification which businesses must attain and can be used in two ways – first, it can be used for internal auditing purposes by the business and, second, it can be used to seek certification or for contractual purposes.

Certification is not undertaken by the ISO but by nationally based independent assessors. There will be periodic visits at six-monthly intervals to check particular aspects of the business's processes and an audit of the whole business is undertaken every three years.

The ISO 9001 is likely to be a familiar concept to in-house lawyers working in commerce and industry having, as it does, a wider coverage than simply legal services providers.

10.2.4 Useful references

- **www.lawsociety.org.uk** – For further details about personal accreditation schemes including fees, assessment providers, etc. Also for information about the Lexcel accreditation scheme.
- **www.sra.org.uk** – For further information about the SRA mandatory accreditation schemes.
- **www.sahca.org.uk** – The Solicitors Association of Higher Court Advocates.
- **www.iso.org** – The International Organization for Standardization.
- **www.gov.uk/government/organisations/office-of-the-immigration-services-commissioner** – The Office of the Immigration Services Commissioner.
- **www.gov.uk/government/organisations/legal-aid-agency** – The Legal Aid Agency.

CHAPTER 11

Troubleshooting – different types of in-house practice

11.1 INTRODUCTION

Using the description 'in-house practice' would suggest that this type of employment is a one-dimensional environment. As will be obvious to anyone working in such a capacity, nothing could be further from the truth. In much the same way that private practice covers a variety of styles of business – nowadays from sole practice through to alternative business structures (ABSs) and everything in between – the same is true of in-house practice.

The role of an in-house solicitor working in a public sector environment will be different from that of an in-house solicitor working in a not-for-profit organisation or in commerce and industry. In the commerce and industry environment, there are extremes, and shades of grey in between, with some lawyers being employed by global financial corporations and similar and others finding themselves as the only lawyer in a much smaller business.

This chapter examines different types of in-house practice and suggests role-specific risk factors and other considerations that should be borne in mind by solicitors working in these particular environments. This is not by reference to risks associated with particular areas of law – the practitioner should be aware of these and have the requisite knowledge to provide a competent service (as required under paragraphs 3.2 and 3.3 of the SRA Code of Conduct for Solicitors, RELs and RFLs). Instead, this chapter flags up the key regulatory issues with particular reference to the requirements of the SRA Standards and Regulations, the impact on the individual's personal position as an authorised person, and particular risks and pitfalls associated with the type of employment.

11.2 LOCAL AUTHORITY AND PUBLIC SECTOR LAWYERS

Local authorities and public sector entities employ a sizeable number of solicitors to fulfil a variety of legal functions in different areas of the law. This is usually through an in-house legal team which is regarded as one of the employer's business units or departments. The local authority lawyer, unlike some other types of in-house solicitors, is likely to be in a working environment with other lawyers and paralegals.

11.2.1 Practising certificates

Local authority solicitors, and others, are entitled to carry on certain advocacy functions without being qualified persons as defined by legislation.

This places in-house lawyers in a difficult personal position: while they can rely on the Local Government Act 1972, s.223, this means that they must not be held out, or be employed as, a solicitor.

Questions

- Are you satisfied that you are not breaching the Solicitors Act 1974?
- If you are relying on the Local Government Act 1972, do you have a record that proper authority has been granted to you and that this is adequately documented in the Council minutes?
- Are you certain that your job description and contract of employment do not create problems?

11.2.2 Client base

Solicitors employed in such a capacity will want to have a clear understanding about which master they serve. This is often an environment where the lawyers find they are expected to provide services over and beyond what is permitted by the SRA.

In terms of local authority employees, the local authority will be their employer and this will mean that the local authority is the in-house solicitor's client. Similarly, with public sector employment, the employer will be the trust, agency, etc. with whom the lawyer has entered into an employment contract. While instructions may be obtained from other employees it will always be important to bear in mind that this will be on the basis of delegated authority and that there may be situations where it is necessary to check the basis of the delegated decision making or deal directly with the elected councillors or similar and obtain appropriate resolutions.

There are restrictions on other clients to whom an employed solicitor can provide legal services. While in-house solicitors are able to provide unreserved services to clients who are not part of their organisation, it is essential that they are satisfied that in doing this they are not acting in breach of the SRA Principles, the SRA Codes of Conduct or any other relevant sections of the SRA Standards and Regulations. It is also essential that the services do not stray into the provision of reserved legal activities. Providing a service such as litigation or conveyancing (i.e. reserved legal activities) to a member of the public from an unauthorised business would be a statutory offence.

11.2.3 Being team leader of the in-house legal team

A common feature of this type of employment is likely to be the fact that you are not the only lawyer employed by the local authority, etc. and that you operate as part of a legal team, which will be one of the business units of the authority or entity. The SRA Standards and Regulations recognise this and create particular duties and responsibilities that are aimed at solicitor-managers/supervisors of other individuals. This is particularly so in the Code for Individuals at paragraphs 3.5 and 3.6.

Such standards carry a level of personal responsibility for the actions of others. Whether or not these are achievable may come down to whether the team leader has the support of other senior officials. At the very least, the senior officials need an understanding of the lawyer's additional obligations.

Questions

- Are you confident that you can demonstrate that members of your team understand the regulatory issues you need to address?
- How is this addressed in their contracts of employment and in your contract and job description?
- Do senior members of the organisation support you in complying with the Standards and Regulations?
- Do you have adequate facilities and resources for regulatory and legal training?

11.2.4 Employment in another capacity

Solicitors are often considered for other roles in such organisations, with many becoming chief executives or chief/senior operating officers.

Questions

- Are you also practising as a solicitor (triggering the need for a practising certificate)?
- If you are a non-practising solicitor, is this clear from your job description, contract, etc.?
- Is your remit clear from your job description?

11.3 LAWYERS WORKING FOR NOT-FOR-PROFIT ORGANISATIONS

Solicitors working for not-for-profit organisations are more likely to act for members of the public but are also more likely to have budgetary constraints for funding for practising certificates, training, etc.

11.3.1 Practising certificates

If you are employed as a lawyer, and/or you are performing reserved legal activities, you will need a current practising certificate.

If you are employed in any other capacity, or have a job title such as caseworker or paralegal, you will need to consider your own personal position, the terms of the Solicitors Act 1974, and whether you must nevertheless be certificated.

Questions

- Are you satisfied about your personal position under the Solicitors Act 1974?
- Will you be able to fulfil the SRA's training requirements in terms of the competency standards training you are required to undertake each year?

11.3.2 Employer versus client base

Solicitors working in not-for-profit and charitable organisations will often have a more diverse client base than other in-house lawyers. With such a client base some of the concerns which may sometimes seem more relevant in private practice will also be an issue here: client conflicts, confidentiality and client care standards spring to mind. It also means that such solicitors are more likely to need to hold client money, which will trigger the need to consider the default prohibitions in the SRA Accounts Rules and the need for them to discuss their position with the SRA.

Questions

- Have you read the requirements of the Code for Individuals and the Accounts Rules and are you satisfied that you can comply with your personal duties?
- Have you identified who you are entitled to provide services to as part of your employment?
- Are you holding client money and, if so, are you confident that this is in circumstances prescribed by the SRA?
- Who can you talk to if you have any concerns about possible conflicts between these personal duties and the terms of your employment?

11.3.3 Being a team leader or having management responsibilities

In-house solicitors in not-for-profit organisations are likely to have a number of staff members to supervise, many of whom will not be legally qualified. Such solicitors will need to consider how they comply with their personal duties in the Code for Individuals.

What would be appropriate in terms of a managerial or supervisory framework is not prescribed but must be appropriate to the size and type of organisation. This could mean that the in-house lawyer with managerial responsibilities will need to negotiate resources to ensure that they and people for whom they have management responsibilities are able to comply with the SRA's requirements.

Questions

- Do you have the support of your employer to create the systems, etc. needed to comply with these requirements?
- Do the team members understand what is expected of them?
- Do you have adequate time to supervise the team members?
- Do you have adequate resources, etc. to ensure that team members have legal and regulatory training?

11.3.4 Public funding and the need for accreditation

Lawyers in not-for-profit centres are likely to undertake more publicly funded work than other in-house lawyers and will need to demonstrate compliance with a quality standard (either Lexcel or the SQM Standard as described in **Chapter 10**). The Legal Aid Agency contract and funding are put at risk where these quality standards are not met, and the in-house lawyer will want to ensure that the employer understands what resources and commitments are needed.

Questions

- How do you ensure that your Legal Aid Agency contract is not put at risk?
- What training of team members is required?
- How much time must you allocate to this and do you have the support of your employer?

11.4 LAWYERS WORKING IN COMMERCE AND INDUSTRY

In-house solicitors in commerce and industry are likely to represent the most diverse cross-section of the in-house community. They are less likely to work with fellow lawyers, more likely to have business and commercial considerations to take into account, and more likely to be working in environments where other regulators have a presence.

11.4.1 Practising certificates

Undoubtedly, if you work in this area you will be employed as a lawyer, or have a job description which conveys this meaning.

Questions

- Do you have a current practising certificate?
- If not, why not? Are you confident that you are not committing a breach of the Solicitors Act 1974?

11.4.2 Who is your client?

Usually, your only client will be your employer and related bodies. You can act for other parties subject to your services being restricted to non-reserved legal services and in compliance with the SRA Principles and the SRA Code of Conduct for Individuals.

Questions

- Are you clear about the identity of your employer/client?
- Are you satisfied that when asked to act for other entities this does not place you in breach of the SRA Standards and Regulations?
- For example, do you check for conduct issues when acting for third parties, e.g. conflict checks, issues with confidentiality and the duty to disclose material information, duties to the court, etc.?
- If you had a problem in reconciling personal regulatory duties with duties owed to your employer, who would you talk to?

11.4.3 Regulatory compliance

Being employed as an in-house solicitor means dual loyalties: first, to the employer and, second, to the SRA who will require you to comply with pertinent aspects of the SRA Standards and Regulations and regulatory requirements.

Questions

- Do you understand the personal duties imposed on you because you are a practising lawyer?
- Are you satisfied that these personal duties can be reconciled with the terms of your employment?
- If there were a conflict, who would you be able to raise your concerns with?
- You cannot hold client money, so does this cause difficulties with what you are being asked to do?

11.4.4 Access to the board

Being an in-house solicitor and an employee triggers the need to consider legislative compliance by the employer. Turning a blind eye to any legislative offence is not an option.

Questions

- How do you ensure that you have access to all areas so that you know what you need to know?
- Who would you talk to if you had concerns that the business, or any individual within it, were breaching legislative requirements or were committing a criminal offence?
- Do you have an adequate mandate to introduce and oversee policies and procedures designed to assist with the risk management of such issues?
- Are you expected to have oversight of corporate governance issues and, if so, do you have the appropriate resources to advise competently?

11.4.5 International perspective

In-house lawyers may find that there is an international dimension to their business which means that they need to consider whether this, and the requirements of overseas legislation and regulatory requirements, are reconcilable with their domestic obligations.

Questions

- Are you satisfied that you understand the issues which are triggered by your business's methods of operation?
- Do you need access to all areas to find out where the pinch points lie?
- What would you do, and who would you approach, if you found pinch points?

11.4.6 The requirements of other regulators

In-house lawyers in the commerce and industry field are more likely to have a link with other regulators than, for example, in-house lawyers working for public authorities. The most obvious example arises in respect of those lawyers in the financial services industry who are employed by businesses that are authorised and regulated by the Financial Conduct Authority (FCA).

Bear in mind that the FCA and the SRA, in common with other regulators, have reciprocity arrangements to share information, and any wrongdoings in terms of FCA compliance may well be shared with the SRA and considered in terms of whether there are any disciplinary issues to address.

Questions

- Do you have a sufficiently good understanding of the rules and requirements of the other regulator?
- Does that create a problem with the personal duties required of you because of your employment as a lawyer?
- If the various requirements cannot be reconciled, who would you be able to discuss your concerns with?
- Will you be expected, because of your legal training, etc., to contribute to the corporate governance arrangements which will be needed to ensure compliance with these other regulatory obligations? If not, what resources and training would you need to be able to perform such a function properly?

11.5 LAWYERS WORKING IN-HOUSE OVERSEAS

The SRA Standards and Regulations allow you to practise as a solicitor from an office outside England and Wales in a number of ways but always subject to compliance with SRA duties and, in particular, the SRA Principles and the SRA Code for Individuals.

11.5.1 Take care with your description

It is important to be aware that certain lawyers of other jurisdictions can use the title 'solicitor'. In much the same way as an Australian solicitor practising in England and Wales could not simply describe themselves as a solicitor without qualifying that description with reference to their home jurisdiction (in order to avoid misleading anyone that they were a solicitor of the Senior Courts of England and Wales), the same is true of English and Welsh solicitors practising overseas.

Questions

- Do you need a practising certificate?
- Do you need to consider the Establishment Directive requirements and the implications of any changes following Brexit?

11.5.2 Can the SRA requirements be reconciled with domestic requirements in the place where you work?

As a solicitor, working in a foreign jurisdiction means that you need to reconcile the personal regulatory issues which you have taken with you from your home jurisdiction with those that apply at your new place of work.

Questions

- Have you considered the local legal and regulatory requirements?
- Who would you talk to within the organisation if there were difficulties in reconciling different duties?

CHAPTER 12

Further resources

12.1 LAW SOCIETY ASSISTANCE

12.1.1 Anti-money laundering

The Law Society offers information and training about anti-money laundering including the Legal Sector Affinity Group Anti-Money Laundering guidance and a free email newsletter.
www.lawsociety.org.uk/advice/anti-money-laundering

12.1.2 Equality and diversity

The Law Society offers advice to firms through its Equality and Diversity Section.
www.lawsociety.org.uk/support-services/practice-management/diversity-inclusion

12.1.3 In-house Division

The In-house Division is the Law Society's online community for in-house lawyers working in the corporate and public sectors, not-for-profit organisations and charities.
https://communities.lawsociety.org.uk/in-house

12.1.4 Junior Lawyers Division (JLD)

The JLD has useful advice and case studies for solicitors considering moving in-house.
https://communities.lawsociety.org.uk/junior-lawyers

12.1.5 Practice Advice Service

The Practice Advice Service offers support and advice on legal practice and procedure. The service is staffed by solicitors who have access to a wide range of information sources and specialists across the Law Society.

Tel: 020 7320 5675 or see online at: **www.lawsociety.org.uk/support-services/help-for-solicitors/practice-advice-service**

12.1.6 Regulation

In its 'Support and Services' section the Law Society offers advice and assistance for COLPs, COFAs and ABSs.
www.lawsociety.org.uk/support-services/risk-compliance/regulation

12.1.7 Risk and Compliance

The Risk and Compliance Service offers help to its members on all aspects of regulatory compliance.
https://communities.lawsociety.org.uk/risk-and-compliance

12.2 OTHER ASSISTANCE

12.2.1 Advisory, Conciliation and Arbitration Service (ACAS)

For information about equality legislation in the business context see the ACAS website:
www.acas.org.uk

12.2.2 Commerce & Industry (C&I) Group

The C&I Group offers advice, training and networking for lawyers working in-house and is an association formed by in-house lawyers for in-house lawyers. The C&I Group also organises free events for its seven regions – London, Central, Yorkshire, Midlands, North West, Thames Valley and Tyne Tees. These range from legal topic seminars to networking events.
www.cigroup.org.uk

12.2.3 Equality and Human Rights Commission

For information about equality legislation in the UK see the website of the Equality and Human Rights Commission:
www.equalityhumanrights.com

12.2.4 Financial Conduct Authority (FCA)

For details about authorisation requirements under the Financial Services and Markets Act 2000 see the FCA website:
www.fca.org.uk

12.2.5 Legal Ombudsman (LeO)

LeO was set up by LSA 2007 to run an independent ombudsman scheme that resolves complaints about lawyers in a fair and effective way.
www.legalombudsman.org.uk

12.2.6 Legal Services Board (LSB)

The LSB is the independent body responsible for overseeing the regulation of lawyers in England and Wales.
www.legalservicesboard.org.uk

12.2.7 Lawyers in Local Government (LLG)

LLG is the representational body for all lawyers and governance officers working in local authorities or similar organisations.
www.lawyersinlocalgovernment.org.uk

LLG offers training via LLG Legal Training: **www.llglegaltraining.org.uk**

12.2.8 Solicitors Regulation Authority (SRA)

For access to the complete online version of the SRA Standards and Regulations, as well as other regulatory advice, see the SRA website:
www.sra.org.uk

12.2.9 National Crime Agency (NCA)

For information about emerging risks see the NCA website:
www.nationalcrimeagency.gov.uk

APPENDIX A

SRA Standards and Regulations (relevant extracts)

APPENDIX A1

SRA Principles [2019]

INTRODUCTION

The SRA Principles comprise the fundamental tenets of ethical behaviour that we expect all those that we regulate to uphold. This includes all individuals we authorise to provide legal services (solicitors, RELs and RFLs), as well as authorised firms and their managers and employees. For licensed bodies, these apply to those individuals, and the part of the body (where applicable), involved in delivering the services we regulate in accordance with the terms of your licence.

Should the Principles come into conflict, those which safeguard the wider public interest (such as the rule of law, and public confidence in a trustworthy solicitors' profession and a safe and effective market for regulated legal services) take precedence over an individual client's interests. You should, where relevant, inform your client of the circumstances in which your duty to the Court and other professional obligations will outweigh your duty to them.

The Principles and Codes are underpinned by our Enforcement Strategy, which explains in more detail our approach to taking regulatory action in the public interest.

This introduction does not form part of the SRA Principles.

THE PRINCIPLES ARE AS FOLLOWS

SRA Principles

You act:

1. in a way that upholds the constitutional principle of the rule of law, and the proper administration of justice.
2. in a way that upholds public trust and confidence in the *solicitors*' profession and in legal services provided by *authorised persons*.
3. with independence.
4. with honesty.
5. with integrity.
6. in a way that encourages equality, diversity and inclusion.
7. in the best interests of each *client*.

SUPPLEMENTAL NOTES

Made by the SRA Board on 30 May 2018.

Made under section 31 of the Solicitors Act 1974, section 9 of the Administration of Justice Act 1985 and section 83 of the Legal Services Act 2007.

APPENDIX A2

SRA Code of Conduct for Solicitors, RELs and RFLs [2019]

INTRODUCTION

The Code of Conduct describes the standards of professionalism that we, the SRA, and the public expect of individuals (solicitors, registered European lawyers and registered foreign lawyers) authorised by us to provide legal services.

They apply to conduct and behaviour relating to your practice, and comprise a framework for ethical and competent practice which applies irrespective of your role or the environment or organisation in which you work (subject to the Overseas Rules which apply to your practice overseas); although paragraphs 8.1 to 8.11 apply only when you are providing your services to the public or a section of the public.

You must exercise your judgement in applying these standards to the situations you are in and deciding on a course of action, bearing in mind your role and responsibilities, areas of practice, and the nature of your clients (which in an in house context will generally include your employer and may include other persons or groups within or outside your employer organisation).

You are personally accountable for compliance with this Code – and our other regulatory requirements that apply to you – and must always be prepared to justify your decisions and actions.

A serious failure to meet our standards or a serious breach of our regulatory requirements may result in our taking regulatory action against you. A failure or breach may be serious either in isolation or because it comprises a persistent or concerning pattern of behaviour. In addition to the regulatory requirements set by us in our Codes, Principles and our rules and regulations, we directly monitor and enforce the requirements relating to referral fees set out in section 56 of the Legal Aid, Sentencing and Punishment of Offenders Act 2012, and provisions relating to anti money laundering and counter terrorist financing, as set out in regulations made by the Treasury as in force from time to time.

All these requirements are underpinned by our Enforcement Strategy. That strategy explains in more detail our views about the issues we consider to be serious, and our approach to taking regulatory action in the public interest.

This introduction does not form part of the SRA Code of Conduct for Solicitors, RELs and RFLs.

CODE OF CONDUCT FOR SOLICITORS, RELS AND RFLS

MAINTAINING TRUST AND ACTING FAIRLY

1.1 You do not unfairly discriminate by allowing your personal views to affect your professional relationships and the way in which you provide your services.

1.2 You do not abuse your position by taking unfair advantage of *clients* or others.

1.3 You perform all *undertakings* given by you, and do so within an agreed timescale or if no timescale has been agreed then within a reasonable amount of time.
1.4 You do not mislead or attempt to mislead your *clients*, the *court* or others, either by your own acts or omissions or allowing or being complicit in the acts or omissions of others (including your *client*).

DISPUTE RESOLUTION AND PROCEEDINGS BEFORE COURTS, TRIBUNALS AND INQUIRIES

2.1 You do not misuse or tamper with evidence or attempt to do so.
2.2 You do not seek to influence the substance of evidence, including generating false evidence or persuading witnesses to change their evidence.
2.3 You do not provide or offer to provide any benefit to witnesses dependent upon the nature of their evidence or the outcome of the case.
2.4 You only make assertions or put forward statements, representations or submissions to the *court* or others which are properly arguable.
2.5 You do not place yourself in contempt of *court*, and you comply with *court* orders which place obligations on you.
2.6 You do not waste the *court's* time.
2.7 You draw the *court's* attention to relevant cases and statutory provisions, or procedural irregularities of which you are aware, and which are likely to have a material effect on the outcome of the proceedings.

SERVICE AND COMPETENCE

3.1 You only act for *clients* on instructions from the *client*, or from someone properly authorised to provide instructions on their behalf. If you have reason to suspect that the instructions do not represent your *client's* wishes, you do not act unless you have satisfied yourself that they do. However, in circumstances where you have legal authority to act notwithstanding that it is not possible to obtain or ascertain the instructions of your *client*, then you are subject to the overriding obligation to protect your *client's* best interests.
3.2 You ensure that the service you provide to *clients* is competent and delivered in a timely manner.
3.3 You maintain your competence to carry out your role and keep your professional knowledge and skills up to date.
3.4 You consider and take account of your *client's* attributes, needs and circumstances.
3.5 Where you supervise or manage others providing legal services:

(a) you remain accountable for the work carried out through them; and
(b) you effectively supervise work being done for *clients*.

3.6 You ensure that the individuals you manage are competent to carry out their role, and keep their professional knowledge and skills, as well as understanding of their legal, ethical and regulatory obligations, up to date.

CLIENT MONEY AND ASSETS

4.1 You properly account to *clients* for any *financial benefit* you receive as a result of their instructions, except where they have agreed otherwise.
4.2 You safeguard money and *assets* entrusted to you by *clients* and others.
4.3 You do not personally hold *client money* save as permitted under regulation 10.2(b)(vii)

of the Authorisation of Individuals Regulations, unless you work in an *authorised body*, or in an organisation of a kind *prescribed* under this rule on any terms that may be *prescribed* accordingly.

REFERRALS, INTRODUCTIONS AND SEPARATE BUSINESSES

5.1 In respect of any referral of a *client* by you to another *person*, or of any third party who introduces business to you or with whom you share your *fees*, you ensure that:

(a) *clients* are informed of any financial or other interest which you or your business or employer has in referring the *client* to another *person* or which an *introducer* has in referring the *client* to you;
(b) *clients* are informed of any fee sharing arrangement that is relevant to their matter;
(c) the fee sharing agreement is in writing;
(d) you do not receive payments relating to a referral or make payments to an *introducer* in respect of *clients* who are the subject of criminal proceedings; and
(e) any *client* referred by an *introducer* has not been acquired in a way which would breach the *SRA's regulatory arrangements* if the person acquiring the *client* were regulated by the *SRA*.

5.2 Where it appears to the *SRA* that you have made or received a *referral fee*, the payment will be treated as a *referral fee* unless you show that the payment was not made as such.

5.3 You only:

(a) refer, recommend or introduce a *client* to a *separate business*; or
(b) divide, or allow to be divided, a *client's* matter between you and a *separate business*;

where the *client* has given informed consent to your doing so.

OTHER BUSINESS REQUIREMENTS

5.4 You must not be a *manager*, *employee*, *member* or *interest holder* of a business that:

(a) has a name which includes the word 'solicitors'; or
(b) describes its work in a way that suggests it is a *solicitors'* firm; unless it is an *authorised body*.

5.5 If you are a *solicitor* who holds a practising certificate, an *REL* or *RFL*, you must complete and deliver to the *SRA* an annual return in the *prescribed* form.

5.6 If you are a solicitor or an *REL* carrying on *reserved legal activities* in a *non-commercial body*, you must ensure that:

(a) the body takes out and maintains indemnity insurance; and
(b) this insurance provides adequate and appropriate cover in respect of the services that you provide or have provided, whether or not they comprise *reserved legal activities*, taking into account any alternative arrangements the body or its *clients* may make.

CONFLICT, CONFIDENTIALITY AND DISCLOSURE

CONFLICT OF INTERESTS

6.1 You do not act if there is an *own interest conflict* or a significant risk of such a conflict.

6.2 You do not act in relation to a matter or particular aspect of it if you have a *conflict of interest* or a significant risk of such a conflict in relation to that matter or aspect of it, unless:

- (a) the *clients* have a *substantially common interest* in relation to the matter or the aspect of it, as appropriate; or
- (b) the *clients* are *competing for the same objective*, and the conditions below are met, namely that:
  - (i) all the *clients* have given informed consent, given or evidenced in writing, to you acting;
  - (ii) where appropriate, you put in place effective safeguards to protect your *clients'* confidential information; and
  - (iii) you are satisfied it is reasonable for you to act for all the *clients*.

CONFIDENTIALITY AND DISCLOSURE

6.3 You keep the affairs of current and former *clients* confidential unless disclosure is required or permitted by law or the *client* consents.

6.4 Where you are acting for a *client* on a matter, you make the *client* aware of all information material to the matter of which you have knowledge, except when:

- (a) the disclosure of the information is prohibited by legal restrictions imposed in the interests of national security or the prevention of crime;
- (b) your *client* gives informed consent, given or evidenced in writing, to the information not being disclosed to them;
- (c) you have reason to believe that serious physical or mental injury will be caused to your *client* or another if the information is disclosed; or
- (d) the information is contained in a privileged document that you have knowledge of only because it has been mistakenly disclosed.

6.5 You do not act for a *client* in a matter where that *client* has an interest adverse to the interest of another current or former *client* of you or your business or employer, for whom you or your business or employer holds confidential information which is material to that matter, unless:

- (a) effective measures have been taken which result in there being no real risk of disclosure of the confidential information; or
- (b) the current or former *client* whose information you or your business or employer holds has given informed consent, given or evidenced in writing, to you acting, including to any measures taken to protect their information.

COOPERATION AND ACCOUNTABILITY

7.1 You keep up to date with and follow the law and regulation governing the way you work.

7.2 You are able to justify your decisions and actions in order to demonstrate compliance with your obligations under the *SRA's regulatory arrangements*.

7.3 You cooperate with the *SRA*, other regulators, ombudsmen, and those bodies with a role overseeing and supervising the delivery of, or investigating concerns in relation to, legal services.

7.4 You respond promptly to the *SRA* and:

(a) provide full and accurate explanations, information and documents in response to any request or requirement; and

(b) ensure that relevant information which is held by you, or by third parties carrying out functions on your behalf which are critical to the delivery of your legal services, is available for inspection by the *SRA*.

7.5 You do not attempt to prevent anyone from providing information to the *SRA* or any other body exercising regulatory, supervisory, investigatory or prosecutory functions in the public interest.

7.6 You notify the *SRA* promptly if:

(a) you are subject to any criminal charge, conviction or caution, subject to the Rehabilitation of Offenders Act 1974;

(b) a *relevant insolvency event* occurs in relation to you; or

(c) if you become aware:

(i) of any material changes to information previously provided to the *SRA*, by you or on your behalf, about you or your practice, including any change to information recorded in the *register*; and

(ii) that information provided to the *SRA*, by you or on your behalf, about you or your practice is or may be false, misleading, incomplete or inaccurate.

7.7 You report promptly to the *SRA*, or another *approved regulator*, as appropriate, any facts or matters that you reasonably believe are capable of amounting to a serious breach of their *regulatory arrangements* by any *person* regulated by them (including you).

7.8 Notwithstanding paragraph 7.7, you inform the *SRA* promptly of any facts or matters that you reasonably believe should be brought to its attention in order that it may investigate whether a serious breach of its *regulatory arrangements* has occurred or otherwise exercise its regulatory powers.

7.9 You do not subject any *person* to detrimental treatment for making or proposing to make a report or providing or proposing to provide information based on a reasonably held belief under paragraph 7.7 or 7.8 above, or paragraph 3.9, 3.10, 9.1(d) or (e) or 9.2(b) or (c) of the SRA Code of Conduct for Firms, irrespective of whether the *SRA* or another approved regulator subsequently investigates or takes any action in relation to the facts or matters in question.

7.10 You act promptly to take any remedial action requested by the *SRA*. If requested to do so by the *SRA* you investigate whether there have been any serious breaches that should be reported to the *SRA*.

7.11 You are honest and open with *clients* if things go wrong, and if a *client* suffers loss or harm as a result you put matters right (if possible) and explain fully and promptly what has happened and the likely impact. If requested to do so by the *SRA* you investigate whether anyone may have a claim against you, provide the *SRA* with a report on the outcome of your investigation, and notify relevant persons that they may have such a claim, accordingly.

7.12 Any obligation under this section or otherwise to notify, or provide information to, the *SRA* will be satisfied if you provide information to your firm's *COLP* or *COFA*, as and where appropriate, on the understanding that they will do so.

WHEN YOU ARE PROVIDING SERVICES TO THE PUBLIC OR A SECTION OF THE PUBLIC

CLIENT IDENTIFICATION

8.1 You identify who you are acting for in relation to any matter.

COMPLAINTS HANDLING

8.2 You ensure that, as appropriate in the circumstances, you either establish and maintain, or participate in, a procedure for handling complaints in relation to the legal services you provide.

8.3 You ensure that *clients* are informed in writing at the time of engagement about:

- (a) their right to complain to you about your services and your charges;
- (b) how a complaint can be made and to whom; and
- (c) any right they have to make a complaint to the *Legal Ombudsman* and when they can make any such complaint.

8.4 You ensure that when *clients* have made a complaint to you, if this has not been resolved to the *client's* satisfaction within 8 weeks following the making of a complaint they are informed, in writing:

- (a) of any right they have to complain to the *Legal Ombudsman*, the time frame for doing so and full details of how to contact the *Legal Ombudsman*; and
- (b) if a complaint has been brought and your complaints procedure has been exhausted:
  - (i) that you cannot settle the complaint;
  - (ii) of the name and website address of an alternative dispute resolution (ADR) approved body which would be competent to deal with the complaint; and
  - (iii) whether you agree to use the scheme operated by that body.

8.5 You ensure that complaints are dealt with promptly, fairly, and free of charge.

CLIENT INFORMATION AND PUBLICITY

8.6 You give *clients* information in a way they can understand. You ensure they are in a position to make informed decisions about the services they need, how their matter will be handled and the options available to them.

8.7 You ensure that *clients* receive the best possible information about how their matter will be priced and, both at the time of engagement and when appropriate as their matter progresses, about the likely overall cost of the matter and any *costs* incurred.

8.8 You ensure that any *publicity* in relation to your practice is accurate and not misleading, including that relating to your charges and the circumstances in which *interest* is payable by or to *clients*.

8.9 You do not make unsolicited approaches to members of the public, with the exception of current or former *clients*, in order to advertise legal services provided by you, or your business or employer.

8.10 You ensure that *clients* understand whether and how the services you provide are regulated. This includes:

- (a) explaining which activities will be carried out by you, as an *authorised person*;

(b) explaining which services provided by you, your business or employer, and any *separate business* are regulated by an *approved regulator*; and
(c) ensuring that you do not represent any business or employer which is not authorised by the *SRA*, including any *separate business*, as being regulated by the *SRA*.

8.11 You ensure that *clients* understand the regulatory protections available to them.

SUPPLEMENTAL NOTES

Made by the SRA Board on 30 May 2018.

Made under sections 31 and 32 of the Solicitors Act 1974, section 89 of, and paragraphs 2 and 3 of Schedule 14 to, the Courts and Legal Services Act 1990 and section 57(2) and (8) of the Legal Aid, Sentencing and Punishment of Offenders Act 2012.

APPENDIX A3

SRA Code of Conduct for Firms [2019]

INTRODUCTION

This Code of Conduct describes the standards and business controls that we, the SRA, and the public expect of firms (including sole practices) authorised by us to provide legal services. These aim to create and maintain the right culture and environment for the delivery of competent and ethical legal services to clients. These apply in the context of your practice: the way you run your business and all your professional activities (subject, if you are a licensed body, to any terms of your licence).

Paragraphs 8.1 and 9.1 to 9.2 set out the requirements of managers and compliance officers in those firms, respectively.

A serious failure to meet our standards or a serious breach of our regulatory requirements may lead to our taking regulatory action against the firm itself as an entity, or its managers or compliance officers, who each have responsibilities for ensuring that the standards and requirements are met. We may also take action against employees working within the firm for any breaches for which they are responsible. A failure or breach may be serious either in isolation or because it comprises a persistent or concerning pattern of behaviour.

In addition to the regulatory requirements set by us in our Codes, Principles and our rules and regulations, we directly monitor and enforce the requirements relating to referral fees set out in section 56 of the Legal Aid, Sentencing and Punishment of Offenders Act 2012, and provisions relating to anti money laundering and counter terrorist financing, as set out in regulations made by the Treasury as in force from time to time.

All of these requirements are underpinned by our Enforcement Strategy, which explains in more detail our views about the issues we consider to be serious, and our approach to taking regulatory action in the public interest.

This introduction does not form part of the SRA Code of Conduct for Firms.

CODE OF CONDUCT FOR FIRMS

MAINTAINING TRUST AND ACTING FAIRLY

1.1 You do not unfairly discriminate by allowing your personal views to affect your professional relationships and the way in which you provide your services.

1.2 You do not abuse your position by taking unfair advantage of *clients* or others.

1.3 You perform all *undertakings* given by you and do so within an agreed timescale or if no timescale has been agreed then within a reasonable amount of time.

1.4 You do not mislead or attempt to mislead your *clients*, the *court* or others, either by your own acts or omissions or allowing or being complicit in the acts or omissions of others (including your *client*).

1.5 You monitor, report and publish workforce diversity data, as *prescribed*.

COMPLIANCE AND BUSINESS SYSTEMS

2.1 You have effective governance structures, arrangements, systems and controls in place that ensure:

(a) you comply with all the *SRA's regulatory arrangements*, as well as with other regulatory and legislative requirements, which apply to you;
(b) your *managers* and employees comply with the *SRA's regulatory arrangements* which apply to them;
(c) your *managers* and *interest holders* and those you employ or contract with do not cause or substantially contribute to a breach of the *SRA's regulatory arrangements* by you or your *managers* or employees;
(d) your *compliance officers* are able to discharge their duties under paragraphs 9.1 and 9.2 below.

2.2 You keep and maintain records to demonstrate compliance with your obligations under the *SRA's regulatory arrangements*.
2.3 You remain accountable for compliance with the *SRA's regulatory arrangements* where your work is carried out through others, including your *managers* and those you employ or contract with.
2.4 You actively monitor your financial stability and business viability. Once you are aware that you will cease to operate, you effect the orderly wind-down of your activities.
2.5 You identify, monitor and manage all material risks to your business, including those which may arise from your *connected practices*.

COOPERATION AND ACCOUNTABILITY

3.1 You keep up to date with and follow the law and regulation governing the way you work.
3.2 You cooperate with the *SRA*, other regulators, ombudsmen and those bodies with a role overseeing and supervising the delivery of, or investigating concerns in relation to, legal services.
3.3 You respond promptly to the *SRA* and:

(a) provide full and accurate explanations, information and documentation in response to any requests or requirements;
(b) ensure that relevant information which is held by you, or by third parties carrying out functions on your behalf which are critical to the delivery of your legal services, is available for inspection by the *SRA*.

3.4 You act promptly to take any remedial action requested by the *SRA*.
3.5 You are honest and open with *clients* if things go wrong, and if a *client* suffers loss or harm as a result you put matters right (if possible) and explain fully and promptly what has happened and the likely impact. If requested to do so by the *SRA* you investigate whether anyone may have a claim against you, provide the *SRA* with a report on the outcome of your investigation, and notify relevant persons that they may have such a claim, accordingly.
3.6 You notify the *SRA* promptly:

(a) of any indicators of serious financial difficulty relating to you;
(b) if a *relevant insolvency event* occurs in relation to you;
(c) if you intend to, or become aware that you will, cease operating as a legal business;
(d) of any change to information recorded in the *register*.

3.7 You provide to the *SRA* an information report on an annual basis or such other period as specified by the *SRA* in the *prescribed* form and by the *prescribed* date.

3.8 You notify the *SRA* promptly if you become aware:

(a) of any material changes to information previously provided to the *SRA*, by you or on your behalf, about you or your *managers*, *owners* or *compliance officers*; and

(b) that information provided to the *SRA*, by you or on your behalf, about you or your *managers*, *owners* or *compliance officers* is or may be false, misleading, incomplete or inaccurate.

3.9 You report promptly to the *SRA*, or another *approved regulator*, as appropriate, any facts or matters that you reasonably believe are capable of amounting to a serious breach of their *regulatory arrangements* by any *person* regulated by them (including you) of which you are aware. If requested to do so by the *SRA*, you investigate whether there have been any serious breaches that should be reported to the *SRA*.

3.10 Notwithstanding paragraph 3.9, you inform the *SRA* promptly of any facts or matters that you reasonably believe should be brought to its attention in order that it may investigate whether a serious breach of its regulatory arrangements has occurred or otherwise exercise its regulatory powers.

3.11 You do not attempt to prevent anyone from providing information to the *SRA* or any other body exercising regulatory, supervisory, investigatory or prosecutory functions in the public interest.

3.12 You do not subject any *person* to detrimental treatment for making or proposing to make a report or providing, or proposing to provide, information based on a reasonably held belief under paragraph 3.9 or 3.10 above or 9.1(d) or (e) or 9.2(b) or (c) below, or under paragraph 7.7 or 7.8 of the SRA Code of Conduct for Solicitors, RELs and RFLs, irrespective of whether the *SRA* or another approved regulator subsequently investigates or takes any action in relation to the facts or matters in question.

SERVICE AND COMPETENCE

4.1 You only act for *clients* on instructions from the *client*, or from someone properly authorised to provide instructions on their behalf. If you have reason to suspect that the instructions do not represent your *client's* wishes, you do not act unless you have satisfied yourself that they do. However, in circumstances where you have legal authority to act notwithstanding that it is not possible to obtain or ascertain the instructions of your *client*, then you are subject to the overriding obligation to protect your *client's* best interests.

4.2 You ensure that the service you provide to *clients* is competent and delivered in a timely manner, and takes account of your *client's* attributes, needs and circumstances.

4.3 You ensure that your *managers* and employees are competent to carry out their role, and keep their professional knowledge and skills, as well as understanding of their legal, ethical and regulatory obligations, up to date.

4.4 You have an effective system for supervising *clients'* matters.

CLIENT MONEY AND ASSETS

5.1 You properly account to *clients* for any *financial benefit* you receive as a result of their instructions, except where they have agreed otherwise.

5.2 You safeguard money and *assets* entrusted to you by *clients* and others.

CONFLICT OF INTERESTS

6.1 You do not act if there is an *own interest conflict* or a significant risk of such a conflict.

6.2 You do not act in relation to a matter or a particular aspect of it if you have a *conflict of interest* or a significant risk of such a conflict in relation to that matter or aspect of it, unless:

(a) the *clients* have a *substantially common interest* in relation to the matter or the aspect of it, as appropriate; or
(b) the *clients* are *competing for the same objective*, and the conditions below are met, namely that:

(i) all the *clients* have given informed consent, given or evidenced in writing, to you acting;
(ii) where appropriate, you put in place effective safeguards to protect your *clients'* confidential information; and
(iii) you are satisfied it is reasonable for you to act for all the *clients*.

CONFIDENTIALITY AND DISCLOSURE

6.3 You keep the affairs of current and former *clients* confidential unless disclosure is required or permitted by law or the *client* consents.

6.4 Any individual who is acting for a *client* on a matter makes the *client* aware of all information material to the matter of which the individual has knowledge except when:

(a) the disclosure of the information is prohibited by legal restrictions imposed in the interests of national security or the prevention of crime;
(b) the *client* gives informed consent, given or evidenced in writing, to the information not being disclosed to them;
(c) the individual has reason to believe that serious physical or mental injury will be caused to the *client* or another if the information is disclosed; or
(d) the information is contained in a privileged document that the individual has knowledge of only because it has been mistakenly disclosed.

6.5 You do not act for a *client* in a matter where that *client* has an interest adverse to the interest of another current or former *client* for whom you hold confidential information which is material to that matter, unless:

(a) effective measures have been taken which result in there being no real risk of disclosure of the confidential information; or
(b) the current or former *client* whose information you hold has given informed consent, given or evidenced in writing, to you acting, including to any measures taken to protect their information.

APPLICABLE STANDARDS IN THE SRA CODE OF CONDUCT FOR SOLICITORS, RELS AND RFLS

7.1 The following paragraphs in the SRA Code of Conduct for Solicitors, RELs and RFLs apply to you in their entirety as though references to 'you' were references to you as a firm:

(a) dispute resolution and proceedings before courts, tribunals and inquiries (2.1 to 2.7);
(b) referrals, introductions and *separate businesses* (5.1 to 5.3); and
(c) standards which apply when providing services to the public or a section of the public, namely client identification (8.1), complaints handling (8.2 to 8.5), and client information and publicity (8.6 to 8.11).

MANAGERS IN SRA AUTHORISED FIRMS

8.1 If you are a *manager*, you are responsible for compliance by your firm with this Code. This responsibility is joint and several if you share management responsibility with other *managers* of the firm.

COMPLIANCE OFFICERS

9.1 If you are a *COLP* you must take all reasonable steps to:

(a) ensure compliance with the terms and conditions of your firm's authorisation;
(b) ensure compliance by your firm and its *managers*, employees or *interest holders* with the *SRA's regulatory arrangements* which apply to them;
(c) ensure that your firm's *managers* and *interest holders* and those they employ or contract with do not cause or substantially contribute to a breach of the *SRA's regulatory arrangements*;
(d) ensure that a prompt report is made to the SRA of any facts or matters that you reasonably believe are capable of amounting to a serious breach of the terms and conditions of your firm's authorisation, or the *SRA's regulatory arrangements* which apply to your firm, *managers* or employees;
(e) notwithstanding sub-paragraph (d), you ensure that the *SRA* is informed promptly of any facts or matters that you reasonably believe should be brought to its attention in order that it may investigate whether a serious breach of its *regulatory arrangements* has occurred or otherwise exercise its regulatory powers,

save in relation to the matters which are the responsibility of the *COFA* as set out in paragraph 9.2 below.

9.2 If you are a *COFA* you must take all reasonable steps to:

(a) ensure that your firm and its *managers* and employees comply with any obligations imposed upon them under the SRA Accounts Rules;
(b) ensure that a prompt report is made to the *SRA* of any facts or matters that you reasonably believe are capable of amounting to a serious breach of the SRA Accounts Rules which apply to them;
(c) notwithstanding sub-paragraph (b), you ensure that the *SRA* is informed promptly of any facts or matters that you reasonably believe should be brought to its attention in order that it may investigate whether a serious breach of its regulatory arrangements has occurred or otherwise exercise its regulatory powers.

SUPPLEMENTAL NOTES

Made by the SRA Board on 30 May 2018.

Made under section 31 of the Solicitors Act 1974, section 9 of the Administration of Justice Act 1985, section 83 of the Legal Services Act 2007, and section 57(2) and (8) of the Legal Aid, Sentencing and Punishment of Offenders Act 2012.

APPENDIX A4

SRA Accounts Rules [2019]

INTRODUCTION

These rules set out our requirements for when firms (including sole practices) authorised by us receive or deal with money belonging to clients, including trust money or money held on behalf of third parties. The rules apply to all firms we regulate, including all those who manage or work within such firms.

Firms will need to have systems and controls in place to ensure compliance with these rules and the nature of those systems must be appropriate to the nature and volumes of client transactions dealt with and the amount of client money held or received.

This introduction does not form part of the SRA Accounts Rules.

PART 1: GENERAL

RULE 1: APPLICATION SECTION

1.1 These rules apply to *authorised bodies*, their *managers* and employees and references to 'you' in these rules should be read accordingly.

1.2 The *authorised body's managers* are jointly and severally responsible for compliance by the *authorised body*, its *managers* and employees with these rules.

1.3 In relation to a *licensed body*, the rules apply only in respect of activities regulated by the *SRA* in accordance with the terms of its licence.

PART 2: CLIENT MONEY AND CLIENT ACCOUNTS

RULE 2: CLIENT MONEY

2.1 '*Client money*' is money held or received by you:

(a) relating to *regulated services* delivered by you to a *client*;

(b) on behalf of a third party in relation to *regulated services* delivered by you (such as money held as agent, stakeholder or held to the sender's order);

(c) as a trustee or as the holder of a specified office or appointment, such as donee of a power of attorney, Court of Protection deputy or trustee of an occupational pension scheme;

(d) in respect of your *fees* and any unpaid *disbursements* if held or received prior to delivery of a bill for the same.

2.2 In circumstances where the only *client money* you hold or receive falls within rule 2.1(d) above, and:

(a) any money held for *disbursements* relates to costs or expenses incurred by you on behalf of your *client* and for which you are liable; and
(b) you do not for any other reason maintain a *client account*;

you are not required to hold this money in a *client account* if you have informed your *client* in advance of where and how the money will be held. Rules 2.3, 2.4, 4.1, 7, 8.1(b) and (c) and 12 do not apply to *client money* held outside of a *client account* in accordance with this rule.

2.3 You ensure that *client money* is paid promptly into a *client account* unless:

(a) in relation to money falling within 2.1(c), to do so would conflict with your obligations under rules or regulations relating to your specified office or appointment;
(b) the *client money* represents payments received from the Legal Aid Agency for your *costs*; or
(c) you agree in the individual circumstances an alternative arrangement in writing with the *client*, or the third party, for whom the money is held.

2.4 You ensure that *client money* is available on demand unless you agree an alternative arrangement in writing with the *client*, or the third party for whom the money is held.

2.5 You ensure that *client money* is returned promptly to the *client*, or the third party for whom the money is held, as soon as there is no longer any proper reason to hold those funds.

RULE 3: CLIENT ACCOUNT

3.1 You only maintain a *client account* at a branch (or the head office) of a *bank* or a *building society* in England and Wales.

3.2 You ensure that the name of any *client account* includes:

(a) the name of the *authorised body*; and
(b) the word 'client' to distinguish it from any other type of account held or operated by the *authorised body*.

3.3 You must not use a *client account* to provide banking facilities to *clients* or third parties. Payments into, and transfers or withdrawals from a *client account* must be in respect of the delivery by you of *regulated services*.

RULE 4: CLIENT MONEY MUST BE KEPT SEPARATE

4.1 You keep *client money* separate from money belonging to the *authorised body*.

4.2 You ensure that you allocate promptly any funds from *mixed payments* you receive to the correct *client account* or business account.

4.3 Where you are holding *client money* and some or all of that money will be used to pay your *costs*:

(a) you must give a bill of *costs*, or other written notification of the costs incurred, to the *client* or the paying party;
(b) this must be done before you transfer any *client money* from a *client account* to make the payment; and
(c) any such payment must be for the specific sum identified in the bill of *costs*, or other written notification of the *costs* incurred, and covered by the amount held for the particular *client* or third party.

RULE 5: WITHDRAWALS FROM CLIENT ACCOUNT

5.1 You only withdraw *client money* from a *client account*:

(a) for the purpose for which it is being held;
(b) following receipt of instructions from the *client*, or the third party for whom the money is held; or
(c) on the *SRA's* prior written authorisation or in *prescribed* circumstances.

5.2 You appropriately authorise and supervise all withdrawals made from a *client account*.
5.3 You only withdraw *client money* from a *client account* if sufficient funds are held on behalf of that specific *client* or third party to make the payment.

RULE 6: DUTY TO CORRECT BREACHES UPON DISCOVERY

6.1 You correct any breaches of these rules promptly upon discovery. Any money improperly withheld or withdrawn from a *client account* must be immediately paid into the account or replaced as appropriate.

RULE 7: PAYMENT OF INTEREST

7.1 You account to clients or third parties for a fair sum of *interest* on any *client money* held by you on their behalf.
7.2 You may by a written agreement come to a different arrangement with the *client* or the third party for whom the money is held as to the payment of *interest*, but you must provide sufficient information to enable them to give informed consent.

RULE 8: CLIENT ACCOUNTING SYSTEMS AND CONTROLS

8.1 You keep and maintain accurate, contemporaneous, and chronological records to:

(a) record in client ledgers identified by the *client's* name and an appropriate description of the matter to which they relate:

(i) all receipts and payments which *client money* on the client side of the client ledger account;
(ii) all receipts and payments which are not *client money* and bills of *costs* including transactions through the *authorised body's* accounts on the business side of the client ledger account;

(b) maintain a list of all the balances shown by the client ledger accounts of the liabilities to *clients* (and third parties), with a running total of the balances; and
(c) provide a cash book showing a running total of all transactions through *client accounts* held or operated by you.

8.2 You obtain, at least every five weeks, statements from *banks*, *building societies* and other financial institutions for all *client accounts* and business accounts held or operated by you.
8.3 You complete at least every five weeks, for all *client accounts* held or operated by you, a reconciliation of the *bank* or *building society* statement balance with the cash book balance and the client ledger total, a record of which must be signed off by the *COFA* or a *manager* of the firm. You should promptly investigate and resolve any differences shown by the reconciliation.

8.4 You keep readily accessible a central record of all bills or other written notifications of *costs* given by you.

PART 3: DEALING WITH OTHER MONEY BELONGING TO CLIENTS OR THIRD PARTIES

RULE 9: OPERATION OF JOINT ACCOUNTS

9.1 If, when acting in a *client's* matter, you hold or receive money jointly with the *client* or a third party, Part 2 of these rules does not apply save for:

(a) rule 8.2 – statements from *banks*, *building societies* and other financial institutions;
(b) rule 8.4 – bills and notifications of *costs*.

RULE 10: OPERATION OF A CLIENT'S OWN ACCOUNT

10.1 If, in the course of practice, you operate a *client's* own account as signatory, Part 2 of these rules does not apply save for:

(a) rule 8.2 – statements from *banks*, *building societies* and other financial institutions;
(b) rule 8.3 – reconciliations;
(c) rule 8.4 – bills and notifications of *costs*.

RULE 11: THIRD PARTY MANAGED ACCOUNTS

11.1 You may enter into arrangements with a *client* to use a *third party managed account* for the purpose of receiving payments from or on behalf of, or making payments to or on behalf of, the *client* in respect of *regulated services* delivered by you to the *client*, only if:

(a) use of the account does not result in you receiving or holding the *client's* money; and
(b) you take reasonable steps to ensure, before accepting instructions, that the *client* is informed of and understands:

  (i) the terms of the contractual arrangements relating to the use of the *third party managed account*, and in particular how any *fees* for use of the *third party managed account* will be paid and who will bear them; and
  (ii) the *client's* right to terminate the agreement and dispute payment requests made by you.

11.2 You obtain regular statements from the provider of the *third party managed account* and ensure that these accurately reflect all transactions on the account.

PART 4: ACCOUNTANTS' REPORTS AND STORAGE AND RETENTION OF ACCOUNTING RECORDS

RULE 12: OBTAINING AND DELIVERY OF ACCOUNTANTS' REPORTS

12.1 If you have, at any time during an *accounting period*, held or received *client money*, or operated a joint account or a *client's* own account as signatory, you must:

(a) obtain an accountant's report for that *accounting period* within six months of the end of the period; and

(b) deliver it to the *SRA* within six months of the end of the *accounting period* if the accountant's report is qualified to show a failure to comply with these rules, such that money belonging to *clients* or third parties is, or has been, or is likely to be placed, at risk.

12.2 You are not required to obtain an accountant's report if:

(a) all of the *client money* held or received during an *accounting period* is money received from the Legal Aid Agency; or

(b) in the *accounting period*, the statement or passbook balance of *client money* you have held or received does not exceed:

(i) an average of £10,000; and

(ii) a maximum of £250,000,

or the equivalent in foreign currency.

12.3 In rule 12.2 above a 'statement or passbook balance' is the total balance of:

(a) all *client accounts* held or operated by you; and

(b) any joint accounts and *clients'* own accounts operated by you,

as shown by the statements obtained under rule 8.2.

12.4 The *SRA* may require you to obtain or deliver an accountant's report to the *SRA* on reasonable notice if you cease to operate as an *authorised body* and to hold or operate a *client account*, or the *SRA* considers that it is otherwise in the public interest to do so.

12.5 You ensure that any report obtained under this rule is prepared and signed by an accountant who is a member of one of the *chartered accountancy bodies* and who is, or works for, a registered auditor.

12.6 The *SRA* may disqualify an accountant from preparing a report for the purposes of this rule if:

(a) the accountant has been found guilty by their professional body of professional misconduct or equivalent; or

(b) the *SRA* is satisfied that the accountant has failed to exercise due care and skill in the preparation of a report under these rules.

12.7 The *SRA* may specify from time to time matters that you must ensure are incorporated into the terms on which an accountant is engaged.

12.8 You must provide to an accountant preparing a report under these rules:

(a) details of all accounts held or operated by you in connection with your practice at any *bank*, *building society* or other financial institution at any time during the *accounting period* to which the report relates; and

(b) all other information and documentation that the accountant requires to enable completion of their report.

12.9 The accountant must complete and sign their report in the *prescribed* form.

RULE 13: STORAGE AND RETENTION OF ACCOUNTING RECORDS

13.1 You must store all *accounting records* securely and retain these for at least six years.

SUPPLEMENTAL NOTES

Made by the SRA Board on 30 May 2018.

Made under sections 32, 33A, 34, 37 of the Solicitors Act 1974, section 9 of the Administration of Justice Act 1985, and section 83(5)(h) of, and paragraph 20 of Schedule 11 to, the Legal Services Act 2007.

APPENDIX B

Lexcel V6.1: Standard for In-house Legal Departments

APPENDIX B1

Lexcel v6.1

ABOUT LEXCEL

With ever-increasing competitive forces and client demands, it's vital to manage the quality and delivery of legal services. A quality management system demonstrates commitment and ability to consistently deliver services that meet client expectations and improve overall satisfaction.

Designed specifically for the legal sector, Lexcel is the Law Society's legal practice quality mark for practice management and client care. It provides a flexible, supportive management framework to help in-house legal departments enhance the service they provide to the wider organisation and in some instances external clients. This includes developing consistent operational efficiencies and client service, managing risk effectively, reducing costs and promoting profitability.

Lexcel defines quality management procedures in seven areas: structure and strategy, financial management, information management, people management, risk management, client care and file and case management.

Achieving accreditation involves the submission of an application form and subsequent assessment by an independent assessment body. Lexcel accreditation is awarded for three years, with annual re-accreditation and monitoring visits to ensure continued compliance.

In-house legal departments are required to achieve and maintain the stated requirements in the Standard. The independent assessment process validates that these have been met.

Lexcel is owned and managed by the Law Society of England and Wales. This includes developing the Standard and associated products, administration and review of all applications, overseeing the assessment process and promoting the scheme. Except where specific franchise agreements are in place, the Law Society of England and Wales is the only body authorised to award Lexcel accreditation.

Who is Lexcel for?

Legal departments in any jurisdiction in the world can apply for accreditation against the Lexcel Standard, regardless of the size or type of work undertaken. See the Scheme rules for further details.

Two versions of Lexcel are available to reflect the needs of domestic and international markets:

- Lexcel England and Wales – version 6.1 of the Standard for legal practices in England and Wales.
- Lexcel International – version 5.1 of the Standard for practices in England and Wales with independent offices overseas and practices in foreign jurisdictions.

Lexcel England and Wales is divided into two versions to meet the needs of legal practices and in-house legal departments. These entities are defined as:

- A law practice in the form of partnerships, limited liability partnerships, sole practitioners, incorporated law firms and alternative business structures (ABSs) authorised and regulated by the Solicitors Regulation Authority (SRA).
- An in-house legal department, including those in corporations, public sector (including ABSs), law centres, not-for-profit and government organisations.

For ease of reference, the generic term 'department' is used throughout the Standard. This refers to any in-house legal team or legal department that is part of a wider organisation.

In-house legal departments with multiple offices can apply by jurisdiction. For example, an in-house legal department with five departments across England and Wales must submit one application and be assessed across all five departments. In contrast, one that has two departments in England and Wales and an independent department overseas would need to submit two applications, if they wanted to apply for Lexcel across multiple jurisdictions. It is not mandatory for all in-house legal departments across a range of jurisdictions to apply for Lexcel. Please see the Scheme rules for further details.

Lexcel can be combined with other quality standards including ISO 9001, Investors in People and the Specialist Quality Mark (SQM) and could reduce the time and cost of assessment. A joint assessment may also be possible.

Lexcel is accepted as a quality standard by the Legal Aid Agency, instead of accreditation against the SQM.

An annual practice registration fee is payable to the Law Society and a fee is also payable to the independent assessment body.

The annual in-house department registration fee is divided into five bands, based on the number of admitted and non-admitted legal advisors in the department:

- 1 legal advisor
- 2–15 legal advisors
- 16–40 legal advisors
- 41–85 legal advisors
- 86+ legal advisors.

Glossary of terms and guidance

Emboldened words (apart from document headings) in the Lexcel Standard are defined in the Glossary of terms.

A main requirement is presented in tabular form in the left-hand column. Specific requirements are listed in the right-hand column as sub-clauses.

Separate Guidance notes provide further explanation of requirements and are divided into general and specific guidance based on whether or not the in-house legal department has external or internal clients.

In-house legal departments have the flexibility to implement procedures that are appropriate to their circumstances in order to meet requirements in the Standard.

Most in-house legal departments will document all procedures in an office manual, but there is no specific requirement that prevents procedures being documented in a number of different sources.

Although Lexcel will help in-house legal departments and organisations comply with some aspects of legislation, accreditation does not guarantee compliance with local laws. This remains the responsibility of the organisation.

Questions?

If, after reading the Standard, Scheme rules and Guidance notes, you have any questions regarding Lexcel, please do not hesitate to contact us:
Tel: +44 (0)20 7320 5933. Email: lexcel@lawsociety.org.uk.

Glossary of terms

Term	Definition
Authorisations	Organisations need to consider whether authorisation **procedures** need to be in place whereby different **personnel** are given permission to approve expenditure to pre-defined levels.
Corporate social responsibility (CSR)	For the purposes of Lexcel, **CSR** is defined as the commitment of an organisation or department to operate in an ethical manner and contribute in a positive way to society. This is an optional requirement for departments, although organisations tendering for the provision of legal services to other organisations may be required to have a **CSR policy** in place.
Evaluation	To make a judgement.
External client(s)	Clients that are not part of the organisation.
Flexible working	**Flexible working** practices have become increasingly relevant to the legal sector as part of recruitment and retention. Some examples of **flexible working** are part time working, annualised hours, compressed hours and remote working.
Malicious software (malware)	Software that is used to disrupt computer operation, gather sensitive data or gain access to private computer systems.
Must	A mandatory requirement.
Objective(s)	Any **objectives** agreed and set out need to be measurable. They will require some form of quantification or have indicators of progress to measure performance.
Personnel	All employed staff and locums.
Plan(s)	A '**plan**' is a documented outline of where an organisation or department desires to be in the future and describes how it intends to arrive at that destination. A **plan** can be described as a map which supports an organisation or a department to arrive at their desired destination in the future. In general, the Lexcel Standard permits organisations or the department to develop **plans** in the manner and detail that the organisation or department considers appropriate, assuming a basic level of adequacy. All **plans must** have a named person who is responsible for the **plan**. They **must** also be reviewed at least annually.
Policy/policies	A '**policy**' is a documented general approach taken within the organisation or department to the issue in question. A **policy** defines why a particular approach is adopted by the organisation or department. All **policies must** have a named person who is responsible for the **policy**. They **must** also be reviewed at least annually.

Procedure(s)	A '**procedure**' is a written description of how an activity will occur within the department or organisation. A **procedure** describes the steps that **personnel** are required to follow in order to complete an activity. At an assessment, a **procedure** can only be said to be complied with if the assessor can observe that the **procedure** contained in the organisation's documentation is in effective operation. All **procedures must** have a named person who is responsible for the **procedure**. They **must** also be reviewed at least annually.
Reasonable adjustments	The duty to make **reasonable adjustments** is a legal responsibility under anti-discrimination legislation. The requirement is intended to make sure that disabled people do not face difficulties in employment, education or when using services. A **reasonable adjustment** is a reasonable step taken to prevent a disabled person suffering a substantial disadvantage compared with people who are not disabled.
Register	Multiple records that are held in hard copy or electronic format.
Risk register	A **risk register** is a record of the risks facing the organisation or department. There is no fixed format for the **risk register** prescribed by Lexcel. It should indicate who has responsibility for a particular risk and any measures taken by the organisation or department to mitigate or reduce the risk.
Role profile	A description of the role undertaken by an individual including the key purpose of the role, summary of responsibilities and the skills and experience required of the individual.
Should	An optional requirement. In some cases, organisations or departments may be required to explain why they have chosen not to implement a requirement by their Lexcel assessor.
Strategic plan	A strategic plan is a plan that defines the organisation's goals and the activities required to achieve those goals.
Supervisor(s)	A person(s) who is (are) of sufficient seniority and in a position of sufficient responsibility with the appropriate skills and experience to guide and assist others.

STANDARD FOR IN-HOUSE LEGAL DEPARTMENTS

1 Structure and strategy		
1.1	The department **must** have documentation setting out the:	a. management structure which designates the responsibilities of individuals and their accountability.
1.2	The department or its organisation **must** have a strategic **plan**. Where the department relies upon their organisation's strategic **plan** this **must** set out the departments' **objectives**. The **plan should** include:	a. **objectives** for at least the next 12 months b. the identification of resources required to meet the **objectives** c. the services the department wishes to offer d. the client groups to be served e. how services will be delivered and marketed f. a documented risk **evaluation** of **objectives** g. **procedures** for regular reporting on performance.
1.3	The organisation **must** have a business continuity **plan** that encompasses the department, which **should** include:	a. an **evaluation** of potential risks that could lead to business interruption b. ways to reduce, avoid and/or transfer the risks c. key people relevant to the implementation of the **plan** d. a **procedure** to test the **plan** annually, to verify that it would be effective in the event of a business interruption.
1.4	The department **should** have a **policy** in relation to **corporate social responsibility**.	
2 Financial management		
2.1	The organisation **must** document the person who has overall responsibility for financial management of the department.	
2.2	The department **should** be able to provide documentary evidence of their financial management **procedure**, including:	a. annual budget including income and expenditure b. variance analysis conducted at least quarterly of income and expenditure against budgets.
2.3	The department **should** have a time recording **procedure**.	
2.4	If appropriate, the department **should** have a **procedure** in relation to billing clients, which **should** include:	a. the frequency and terms for billing clients b. credit limits for new and existing clients c. debt management.
2.5	Departments handling financial transactions **should** have a **procedure**, which **should** include:	a. the transfer of funds b. the management of funds received by the department c. **authorisations**.

3 Information management		
3.1	The department or the organisation **must** have a **policy** to manage personal data which ensures compliance with data protection legislation, which **should** include:	a. the appointment of an appropriate person of sufficient seniority and authority who is responsible for data protection within the department and to liaise with the organisation's Data Protection Officer (DPO) or other person, if one exists b. keeping appropriate records of processing activities and additionally, the lawful basis for processing categories of data and providing information to data subjects including information about data transfers to third countries c. a **procedure** for data subject access requests d. a **procedure** to manage and report data breaches e. regular data protection training for all staff f. a **policy** for reviewing processing operations in light of the obligation of data protection by design and default, which **should** include: i) a **procedure** for identifying when a data protection privacy impact assessment should be carried out g. a **procedure** for identifying and periodically reviewing data retention timescales.
3.2	The department or the organisation **must** have an information management and security **policy** and **should** be accredited against Cyber Essentials. The **policy should** incorporate the following controls:	a. a **register** of relevant information assets b. **procedures** for the protection and security of the information assets c. **procedures** for the retention and disposal of information d. the use of firewalls e. **procedures** for the secure configuration of network devices f. **procedures** to manage user accounts g. **procedures** to detect and remove **malicious software** h. a **register** of all software used i. training for **personnel** on information security j. a **plan** for the updating and monitoring of software.
3.3	The organisation **must** have an email **policy** that encompasses the department, or the department **must** have its own **policy**, which **should** include:	a. the scope of permitted and prohibited use b. **procedures** for monitoring **personnel** using email c. **procedures** for the storage and destruction of emails.

3.4	If the department is featured on the organisation's website, the department **must** be encompassed by the organisation's website management **policy**, which **must** include:	a. consideration of accessibility requirements for disabled clients and **should** include: b. a **procedure** for content approval, publishing and removal c. the scope of permitted and prohibited content d. **procedures** for the management of its security.
3.5	The organisation **must** have an internet access **policy** that encompasses the department, or the department **must** have a **policy** that is particular to their department, this **should** include:	a. the scope of permitted and prohibited use b. **procedures** for monitoring **personnel** accessing the internet.
3.6	If the department participates in social media, the organisation **must** have a social media **policy** that encompasses the department, or the department **must** have its own **policy**, which **should** include:	a. a **procedure** for participating in social media on behalf of the organisation b. the scope of permitted and prohibited content.
3.7	The organisation or department **must** have:	a. a **register** of each **plan**, **policy** and **procedure** that is contained in the Lexcel Standard b. the named person responsible for each **policy**, **plan** and **procedure** that is contained in the Lexcel Standard c. a **procedure** for the review of each **policy**, **plan** and **procedure** that is contained in the Lexcel Standard.
4	**People management**	
4.1	The department or the organisation **must** have a health and safety **policy**.	
4.2	The department or the organisation **must** have an equality and diversity **policy**, which **should** include:	a. recruitment, selection and progression b. a **procedure** to deal with complaints and disciplinary issues in breach of the **policy** c. a **procedure** to monitor diversity and collate equality data d. training of all **personnel** on compliance with equality and diversity requirements e. **procedures** for **reasonable adjustments** for **personnel**.
4.3	The department **must** be encompassed by the organisation's learning and development **policy**, which **should** include:	a. ensuring that appropriate training is provided to **personnel** b. ensuring that all **supervisors** and managers receive appropriate training c. a **procedure** to evaluate training d. a learning and development **plan** for all **personnel**.

4.4	The organisation or department **must** list the tasks to be undertaken by all **personnel** within the department usually in the form of a **role profile**.	
4.5	The department **must** be encompassed by the organisation's **procedures** to deal effectively with recruitment selection and progression, or have **procedures** particular to the department, which **should** include:	a. the identification of vacancies b. the drafting of the job documentation c. methods of attracting candidates d. clear and transparent selection e. storage, retention and destruction of records f. references and ID checking g. where appropriate, the checking of disciplinary records.
4.6	The department **must** be encompassed by the organisation's induction arrangements for **personnel**, or have arrangements particular to the department, including those transferring roles within the organisation and **should** cover:	a. the management structure and the individual's responsibilities b. terms and conditions of employment c. immediate training requirements d. key **policies**.
4.7	The department or their organisations **must** have a **procedure** which details the steps to be followed when a member of **personnel** ceases to be an employee, which **should** include:	a. the handover of work b. exit interviews c. the return of property belonging to the organisation.
4.8	The department **must** be encompassed by the organisation's performance management **policy** or have a **policy** that is particular to the department, which **should** include:	a. the organisation or department's approach to performance management b. performance review periods and timescales.
4.9	The department or the organisations **must** have a whistleblowing **policy**.	
4.10	The department or the organisations **must** have a **flexible working policy**.	
5	**Risk management**	
5.1	The department **must** be encompassed by the organisation's risk management **policy**, or have a **policy** that is particular to the department, which **should** include:	a. a compliance **plan**, if relevant b. a **risk register** c. defined risk management roles and responsibilities d. arrangements for communicating risk information.

5.2	The department **must** be encompassed by the organisation's outsourced activities **policy** or have a **policy** that is particular to the department, which **should** include:	a. details of all outsourced activities including providers b. **procedures** to check the quality of outsourced work c. **procedures** to ensure providers have taken appropriate precautions to ensure information will be protected.
5.3	There **must** be a named **supervisor** for each area of work undertaken by the department.	
5.4	The department **must** have **procedures** to manage instructions which may be undertaken even though they have a higher **risk profile**, including unusual supervisory and reporting requirements or contingency planning.	
5.5	The department **should** maintain lists of work that it will and will not undertake. This information **should** be communicated to all relevant **personnel** and **should** be updated when changes occur.	
5.6	If the department acts or advises **external clients**, they **must** maintain details of the generic risks and causes of claims associated with the area(s) of work undertaken by the department. This information **must** be communicated to all relevant **personnel**.	
5.7	The department **must** have a **procedure** to monitor key dates, or be encompassed by the organisation's **procedure**, which **must** include:	a. the definition of key dates by work type for the department b. ensuring that key dates are recorded on the file and in a back-up system.
5.8	The department **must** be encompassed by the organisation's **policy** on the handling of conflicts, or have a **policy** that is particular to the department, which **should** include:	a. the definition of conflicts b. training for all relevant **personnel** to identify conflicts c. steps to be followed when a conflict is identified.

5.9	The department **must** be encompassed by the organisation's **procedure** to ensure that all **personnel**, both permanent and temporary, are actively supervised, or have **procedures** that are particular to their department. Such **procedures must** include:	a. checks on incoming and outgoing correspondence, where appropriate b. departmental, team and office meetings and communication structures, where appropriate c. reviews of matter details in order to ensure good financial controls and the appropriate allocation of workloads, where appropriate d. the exercise of devolved powers in publicly funded work, where appropriate e. the availability of a **supervisor** f. allocation of new work and reallocation of existing work, if necessary.
5.10	The department **must** have a **procedure** to ensure that all those doing legal work check their files regularly for inactivity.	
5.11	The department **must** have a **procedure** for regular, independent file reviews of either the management of the file or its substantive legal content, or both. In relation to file reviews, the department **must**:	a. define and explain file selection criteria b. define and explain the number and frequency of reviews c. retain a record of the file review on the matter file and centrally d. ensure any corrective action, which is identified in a file review, is acted upon within 28 days and verified e. ensure that the designated **supervisor** reviews and monitors the data generated by file reviews f. conduct a review at least annually of the data generated by file reviews.

5.12	Operational risk **must** be considered and recorded in all matters before, during and after the processing of instructions. Before the matter is undertaken the legal advisor **must**:	a. consider if a new client and/or matter is accepted by the department, in accordance with section 6.1 and 6.7 below b. assess the risk profile of all new instructions and notify the **supervisor**, in accordance with **procedures** under 5.4, of any unusual or high risk considerations in order that appropriate action may be taken. During the retainer the legal advisor **must**: c. consider any change to the **risk profile** of the matter and report and advise on such circumstances without delay, informing the **supervisor** if appropriate d. inform the client in all cases where an adverse costs order is made against the organisation in relation to the matter in question. At the end of the matter the legal advisor **must**: e. undertake a concluding risk assessment by considering if the client's **objectives** have been achieved f. notify the **supervisor** of all such circumstances in accordance with documented **procedures** in section 5.4 above.

5.13 If anti-money laundering legislation applies to the organisation, the department **must** be encompassed by the organisation's **policy** to mitigate and manage money laundering and terrorist financing risks and to ensure compliance with anti-money laundering (AML) legislation, or have a **policy** that is particular to the department. The **policy should** be approved by senior management and **must** include:	a. a documented risk assessment that identifies and assesses the risks of money laundering and terrorist financing to which the department is subject b. the appointment of a nominated officer usually referred to as a Money Laundering Reporting Officer (MLRO) c. a **procedure** for making disclosures within the organisation and by the MLRO to the authorities d. a **procedure** for checking the identity of the department's clients, if appropriate e. a **plan** for the training of **personnel** f. **procedures** for the proper maintenance of records g. a system for responding rapidly to AML enquiries from the authorities h. where appropriate with regard to the size and nature of the department: i) appoint a person of sufficient seniority as the officer responsible for the department's compliance with the current money laundering regulations ii) ensure that the organisation carries out screening of relevant employees iii) establish an independent audit function to evaluate, monitor compliance with and improve the effectiveness of the organisation's AML policies, controls and procedures if no such function exists within the organisation. Otherwise, the department **must** document why 5.13h(i–iii) above are not appropriate.
5.14 The department **must** be encompassed by the organisation's **policy** setting out the **procedures** to prevent bribery in accordance with current legislation or have a **policy** particular to the department.	
5.15 The department **should** have a **policy** setting out the **procedures** to prevent facilitation of criminal tax evasion by associated persons in accordance with current legislation.	

5.16 The department **must** be included in the organisation's analysis of risk assessment data that is generated or undertake an analysis of risk data particular to their department. This **should** include:	a. any indemnity insurance claims (where applicable) b. an analysis of client complaints trends c. data generated by file reviews d. any breaches that have been notified to the SRA e. situations where the department acted where a conflict existed (where applicable) f. the identification of remedial action g. risk of non-compliance with current policy to manage personal data.
6 Client care	
6.1 The department **must** have a **policy** for client care, which **should** include:	a. how enquiries from potential clients will be dealt with b. ensuring that before taking on a client, the department has sufficient resources and competence to deal with the matter c. protecting client confidentiality, including their data protection rights d. a timely response is made to telephone calls and correspondence from the client and others e. a **procedure** for referring clients to third parties f. the provision of **reasonable adjustments** for disabled clients.

6.2 The department **must** communicate the following to clients in writing, unless an alternative form of communication is deemed more appropriate:	a. where appropriate, establish the client's requirements and **objectives** b. provide a clear explanation of the issues involved and the options available to the client c. explain what the legal advisor will and will not do d. agree with the client the next steps to be taken e. keep the client informed of progress, as agreed f. establish in what timescale that matter will be dealt with g. where appropriate, establish the method of funding h. where appropriate, consider whether the intended action would be merited on a cost benefit analysis i. agree an appropriate level of service j. explain the department's responsibilities and the client's k. provide the client with the name and status of the person dealing with their matter l. where appropriate, provide the client with the name and status of the person responsible for the overall supervision of their matter m. where appropriate, explain to the client their rights as data subjects and provide the client with the name of the person responsible for data protection.
6.3 Where appropriate, the department **should** have a service level or similar agreement with their client departments. There **should** be a **procedure** to regularly review such agreements to ensure they are in plain English.	

6.4	Where appropriate, the department **must** give clients the best information possible about the likely overall cost of the matter, both at the outset and when appropriate, as the matter progresses, in particular the department **should**:	a. advise the client of the basis of the department's charging b. advise the client where the organisation will receive a financial benefit as a result of accepting instructions c. advise the client if the charging rates are to be increased d. advise the client of likely payments which the department or the client may need to make to others e. discuss with the client how they will pay f. advise the client that there are circumstances where the department may be entitled to exercise a lien for unpaid costs g. advise the client of their potential liability for any other party's costs.
6.5	The department **must** be encompassed by the organisation's complaints handling **procedure** or have a **procedure** particular to the department, which **should** include:	a. the definition of what the organisation regards as a complaint b. informing the client at the outset of the matter, that in the event of a problem they are entitled to complain c. the name of the person with overall responsibility for complaints d. providing the client with a copy of the organisation's or department's complaints procedure, if requested e. once a complaint has been made, the person complaining is informed in writing: i) how the complaint will be handled; and ii) in what time they will be given an initial and/or substantive response f. recording and reporting centrally all complaints received from clients g. identifying the cause of any problems of which the client has complained, offering any appropriate redress, and correcting any unsatisfactory procedures.
6.6	The department **must** be encompassed by the organisation's **procedure** to monitor client satisfaction or have a **procedure** that is particular to the department.	
6.7	Where appropriate, the department **must** have a **procedure** to accept or decline instructions, which should include:	a. how decisions are made to accept instructions from new and existing clients b. how decisions are made to stop acting for an existing client c. how decisions are made to decline instructions.

7 File and case management	
7.1 The department **must** ensure that the strategy for a matter is always apparent on the matter file and that in complex cases a project plan is developed.	
7.2 The department **must** document **procedures** for the giving, monitoring and discharge of undertakings.	
7.3 The department **must** be encompassed by the organisation's **procedure** or have a **procedure** particular to the department to:	a. list open and closed matters b. ensure that they are able to identify and trace any documents, files, deeds, wills or any other items relating to the matter c. safeguard the confidentiality of matter files and all other client information d. ensure that the status of the matter and the action taken can be easily checked by other members of the department e. ensure that documents are stored on the matter file(s) in an orderly way.
7.4 The department will have **procedures** to ensure that matters are progressed in an appropriate manner. In particular:	a. key information **must** be recorded on the file b. a timely response is made to telephone calls and correspondence from the client and others c. where appropriate, continuing cost information is provided d. clients are informed in writing if the person with conduct of their matter changes, or there is a change of person to whom any problem with service may be addressed.

7.5	The department **must** be encompassed by the organisation's documented **procedure** for using barristers, expert witnesses and other external advisers who are involved in the delivery of legal services, or have a **procedure** particular to the department, which **should** include provision for the following:	a. use of clear selection criteria in line with the equality and diversity **policy** b. where appropriate, consult with the client in relation to selection of advocate or other professional c. advising the clients of the name and status of the person being instructed, how long she/he might take to respond and, where disbursements are to be paid by the client, the cost involved d. maintenance of records on barristers and experts used, including evidence of assessment against the criteria e. **evaluation** of performance, for the information of other members of the department or organisation f. giving clear instructions g. checking of opinions and reports received to ensure they adequately provide the information sought (and, in litigation matters, comply with the rules of court and any court orders) h. payment of fees.
7.6	The department **must** have **procedures** to ensure that, at the end of the matter, the department:	a. if required, reports to the client on the outcome and explains any further action that the client is required to take in the matter and what (if anything) the department will do b. where appropriate, accounts to the client for any outstanding money c. returns to the client any original documents or other property belonging to the client, if required d. if appropriate, advises the client about arrangements for storage and retrieval of papers and other items retained (in so far as this has not already been dealt with, for example, in terms of business) and any charges to be made in this regard e. advises the client whether it is appropriate to review the matter in future and, if so, when and why f. archives and destroys files in an appropriate manner.

Index